# Abundance by Design

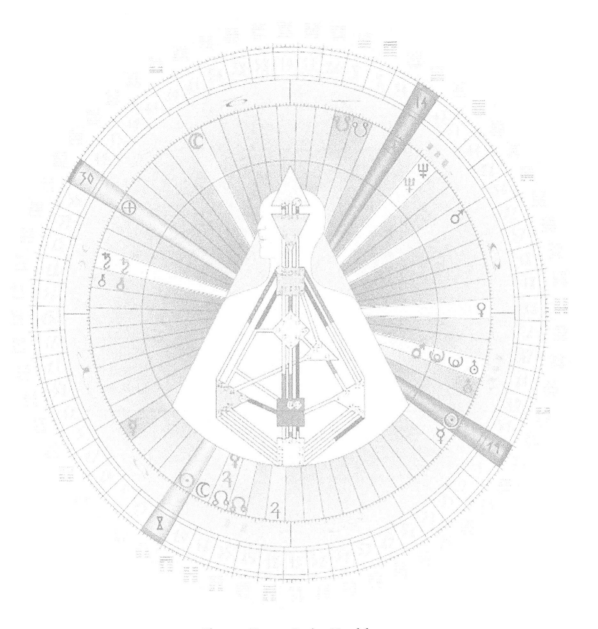

Figure 1. Human Design Mandala

# Abundance By Design:

## Life By Human Design Series, Volume 1;

Discover Your Unique Code for Health, Wealth and Happiness with Human Design

## Karen Curry Parker

### And Human Design Experts:

| | | |
|---|---|---|
| Linda Bisson Copp | Peg Rose Goddard | Evelyn Levenson |
| Dave Buck | Rebekkah Hanson | Kristin Shorter |
| Linda Grace Farley | Alana Heim | Lorie Speciale |
| Tina Forsyth | Sandra Lee | Quay Whitlock |

**GracePoint Matrix, LLC., Publishing Division**

First Digital Edition

Printed in the United States

Publisher's Cataloging-in-Publication Data
provided by Five Rainbows Cataloging Services

Names: Hilliard, Heather M., editor.
Title: Abundance by design : discover your unique code for health, wealth and happiness with human design / [edited by] Heather M. Hilliard ; [written by] Karen Curry Parker [and 12 others].
Description: First edition. | Colorado Springs, CO : GracePoint Matrix, 2016. | Series: Life by human design, vol. 1.
Identifiers: LCCN 2016954478 | ISBN 978-0-9976035-0-7 (pbk.) | ISBN 978-0-9976035-1-4 (ebook)
Subjects: LCSH: Astrology. | Self-realization. | Self-actualization (Psychology). | Conduct of life. | Motivation (Psychology) | BISAC: BODY, MIND & SPIRIT / Astrology / General. | SELF-HELP / Motivational & Inspirational.
Classification: LCC BF1708.1 A28 2016 (print) | LCC BF1708.1 (ebook) | DDC 133.5--dc23.

Legal Notices:

Some names and identifying details have been changed to protect the privacy of individuals.

This book is not intended as a substitute for the medical advice of physicians or qualified therapists. The reader should regularly consult a physician in matters relating to his/her health and particularly with respect to any symptoms that may require diagnosis or medical attention.

Thanks and appreciation to our:

Editor: Heather M. Hilliard,
Production Coordinator: Camille Y. Truman

ISBN 978-0-9976035-0-7

# Table of Contents

# List of Figures

# Karen Curry Parker

# Introduction

As a life coach, writer and human potential expert for the last 25 years, I've worked with a lot of enlightened people who have been willing to really do the work and show up for their lives in a big, inspired way.

They've taken every workshop they can, have lives full of books, gone to therapy, hired coaches, studied and learned every success strategy they can. Yet, they can't quite create the abundance they're seeking in their lives.

Oh sure, they can get it to work sometimes and maybe even reach a comfortable minimum. But, ultimately (in spite of all their efforts), they really haven't quite tapped into the juice, the joy or the vitality that an inspired, abundant, and awakened life promises.

Does this sound familiar?

If this sounds like you, you are not alone.

I've been a personal growth and development junkie for most of my adult life. My desire to master abundance and success was born strictly out of desperation. At the age of 38, after years of struggling with my first marriage and finances, I became a full-time single mother of four children; I was bankrupt and experienced deep financial terror.

I "knew" what I needed to do. I had been studying every abundance program I could find, I went to every workshop and training I could reach. I had vision boards all over my wall, wrote hundreds of affirmations in my journal, and made "mind" movies on my computer. I even wrote my intentions on my hand with a red felt tip marker every morning.

However, I still struggled mightily, robbing Peter to pay Paul, narrowly avoiding the repo man (on most months) managing to eek through each day, watching every penny. Along the way, my house was foreclosed, had my car repossessed and a variety of other pretty serious financial misadventures occurred, too.

I was a new student of Human Design in those days. I had learned about Human Design from my first husband before our divorce. He had brought a Human Design chart back from a spiritual retreat in Sedona, Arizona. When I first saw that strange "triangle" with all those shapes and lines, I cried. There was something so compelling in that chart for me. It was something deeply familiar and profound.

When I got my own Human Design chart a few days later, I discovered that I was a Manifesting Generator Type. As a Manifesting Generator, the best way for me to make decisions and use my energy properly is to wait for something to show up in my life and then, in response, do the things that feel good.

As I was gaining mastery, I soon found out that the process of learning how to wait and doing what feels good proved to be quite challenging! I had never waited for anything in my entire life! I was a doer, a go-getter, a "manifest my own destiny" kind of gal.

I was also deeply accustomed to taking the most difficult path and suffering along the way. As comical as it sounds, doing what felt good left me feeling confused and guilty. I felt certain that if I followed my bliss, I was surely lacking in character and probably taking something away from someone else.

The whole Human Design thing seemed a little wacky, but I was willing to explore and experiment with it. Within weeks of getting my chart, I felt compelled to uproot my family and move to Sedona, Arizona so that I could study more about Human Design. The headquarters for Human Design, at that time, was located there and it was my hope that I could work at the office to learn everything I could about Human Design.

Shortly after arriving in Sedona, my youngest son fell ill with an ear infection. After taking him to the doctor, I walked out of the pediatrician's office and noticed the Human Design "triangle" on the door across the hall. To go through that door felt so right so I scooped up my kid onto my hip and walked into that office.

Sitting at the desk facing the door was a blonde woman with a big smile. She asked me if I'd come about the job. My inner response was electrical; I said, "Yes" before I even could think about it. I was "home" and my journey to learning more about Human Design had started.

I had waited (albeit for a very short time) and something "showed up" in my life. It felt good so I jumped into action and responded to the opportunity.

In the process of learning more about Human Design, my marriage finally fell apart and my finances (which weren't great during my marriage), became even more tenuous. I was left with full-time custody and financial responsibility for my children after our divorce.

While all of this was unfolding, I was desperately trying to find answers to my money problems. I had grown up in an entrepreneurial family so I was no stranger to working in an innovative and self-sustaining way. Somehow, no matter how hard I worked, I never really created the money I needed and dreamed of.

I voraciously gobbled up any and all abundance teachings. Even though I knew that Human Design told me I should "wait" and see what appears, I felt an enormous amount of pressure to keep taking some kind of action. Waiting felt like failing and, even though I knew better, I kept pushing.

I watched other people at the abundance seminars leap up in the middle of the training and run to the back of the room, credit cards held up high in the air as they scrambled to take advantage of "limited time offers." They would purchase exclusive training packages with various wealth gurus in spite of the fact these new "clients" didn't know how they would find the money for their next house payment.

I was fascinated as the energy of the room inspired me and my fellow attendees to make fast choices in the heat of the moment, pressured to buy more and just "frickin' do it." I went home from these weekends determined to apply all the new things I had learned only to lose my steam and motivation a couple of days after the training.

I felt like a failure, like I had no willpower and that I was weak. I couldn't understand where my momentum went. I didn't see why I couldn't focus my inspiration or keep my motivation flowing in a sustainable way.

But that didn't stop me from continuing to try.

Finally, after the very last abundance seminar I ever attended in my life, I came home determined to just "make my destiny" happen. I wanted to teach Human Design and build a career doing Human Design readings. So, I booked a hotel room, scheduled a seminar to teach people about Human Design, made flyers that I posted all over town, wrote a press release and announced my workshop in the local newspaper.

Mind you, I didn't wait for anything in my outer world to indicate to me that this was the right thing to do. I initiated this whole experience. And I pushed hard. I cold called potential leads (something that felt TERRIBLE, but I did it anyway...), I called the newspaper repeatedly trying to get them to write an article about me. This was all to no avail, but that didn't stop me. I was going to teach this workshop and nothing was going to get in the way of my success.

On the night of the event, I packed up my handouts, my computer, my printer and my signs, headed to the hotel room only to find that I didn't have a single student. Not one.

Shattered, I slunk home. I had wasted energy, time and money that I didn't have to host this workshop. I'd been brave, focused and intentional. I'd affirmed, visualized and trusted. And I failed. Again.

That night, I crawled into the hammock in my back yard after I tucked my kids in bed. I stared up at the amazing, sparkling sky and just surrendered everything. I felt so broken. I had no idea what to do next, where I could earn the money I needed to support my family and how to make my dream into my reality.

I had no option except to surrender and see what happened. No amount of rolling things over and over and over in my mind was revealing to me any kind of answer or giving me any kind of clarity.

I had no choice but to wait. Respond to what materialized.

It didn't take long. People began asking me for Human Design readings and I was eager to share. The response was huge. I was struck repeatedly by how healing the Human Design readings were and also by their accuracy. After one particularly intense Human Design session, my client leaned across the table, stared at me and said, "Karen, you need to teach a workshop about Human Design. This is powerful stuff!"

Her words sent a vibration humming through my heart. Suddenly, I had an action that came to me for response! It wasn't me pushing my seminar, but a suggestion coming to me. I had a deep and resounding inner "YES" and decided to conduct an experiment.

I decided to teach the exact same (unsuccessful) workshop I had planned to teach previously. I booked the same hotel room, re-created the same flyers (with the new date), re-sent the same press release (with the new date), called the newspapers and started spreading the word.

This time, they published the event in the paper; people kept calling and registering. On the night of the workshop, I had 32 people in the room. At that point in my life, it was the most amount of money I'd ever made teaching a workshop!

Two workshops. Two exact same intentions and marketing strategies. One a failure and one a massive success. The only difference is that I pushed to create the failed workshop and I waited for responding to a suggestion for the second.

This understanding created a revolution for me. I began to trust the flow of abundance in my life and I eagerly waited to see what the universe brought me for response. In the mornings I'd start my day following the energy of what felt good and inspiring, even if it meant not doing the things my mind told me I "should" be taking handling. I allowed Life to show me what it wanted me to do instead of allowing my life to be driven by my mind and my belief systems.

Now, I'm not going to lie and say that I never struggled again and every day was joy, abundance and bliss. That would be a lie and an unnatural way to experience life. The Human Design chart shows us is that joy, real joy, is experienced when we fall down and pick ourselves back up repeatedly. The chart also shows us that we have to struggle sometimes to learn.

But we're not designed to suffer.

We are also not designed to push and dictate the unfolding of our lives.

We are designed to *be* and live our lives authentically. When we live our lives from that deep, rich authentic place that only you (as the once-in-a-lifetime-creation you are) can live, Life brings us so many wonderful things — love, abundance, support, power, vitality and opportunities for us to be who we really are.

We are also designed to have our destinies and our life path brought forward to unfold for us. You don't have to figure it out! When you let go, it all unfolds. It's counterintuitive but, 16 years later, I have learned from experimenting over and over again. As you let go and let Life unfold while staying out of the crazy-making of your mind, answers and opportunities reveal themselves to you.

We are all uniquely designed and created. In the Human Design System there are five Energy Types, twelve Profiles, nine Energy Centers, thirty-two Channels, sixty-four Gates, and one hundred ninety-six Incarnation Crosses. What's more, each Gate has the possibility of appearing in one of six Lines. The combination of all of these factors and more in your individual Human Design chart make you a truly unique creation.

And if we are all so astonishingly distinctive, how is it possible that there can be a one-size-fits-all formula for success and abundance?

I'm going to be very bold and state that THERE IS NO ONE SIZE FITS ALL FORMULA FOR SUCCESS AND ABUNDANCE.

Perhaps you've bought into the story of "the" secret to creating success, you've been following all of the steps you've learned and you still haven't experienced the results you expected. It's not your fault. The story we've been told is false. There are more than seven billion ways to be successful on the planet and there is only one way that's right for you. Your way.

Isn't it time to write a new story — your own story — where you create the success and abundance you deserve in the way that is right for you?

In this book, I want to share with you a collection of success stories from people who have courageously stepped out of the old formula for prosperity and have embraced their own unique way of creating success using Human Design.

I also want to share with you information to help you discover your unique way of creating an inspired, abundant life. I will show you the beauty of who you truly are and how other people's energy may have been keeping you from tapping into your beauty. It's exactly what you need to do to discover your unique path to abundance - in the way that's right for you!

If you've ever felt that you're not lovable, abundant, vital, supported, powerful, purposeful and valuable, this book will help you discover that the opposite is Truth.

To get started you will need your Free Human Design chart. To get your Free Chart, please visit GracePoint Matrix.

Once you have your chart read through each chapter, including the stories of the people who have experienced Human Design for themselves, understand how their stories can help and guide you, then continue to work through the exercises in the following chapters so the story of your own abundant life can unfold.

Before we can talk about how you can access your abundance in the way that's right for you, we have to do an overview of what I call the "grammar" of abundance. There are laws of manifesting rooted in quantum physics that dictate how you can create what you want in your life. The basic premise of these rules is that what you put energy into is what creates growth and expansion in your life. Your focused thoughts, actions and emotions create your perception and experience of reality. This basic quantum physics principle is sometimes referred to as the Law of Attraction.

The Law of Attraction is universal and applies to us all, but the way in which you interface with this law will be unique to you, depending on your Human Design.

There are six basic tenets to creating abundance:

    1. You have to know what you want.

    2. You have to believe you can have it.

    3. You have to take guided action to get it.

4. What you pay attention to with your mind and your actions will grow and expand.

5. Your emotions create a specific energetic vibration. Emotions are the source of your most potent creative power.

6. You attract into your life experiences and opportunities that are in alignment with your emotional vibration.

These concepts are illustrated in the model below:

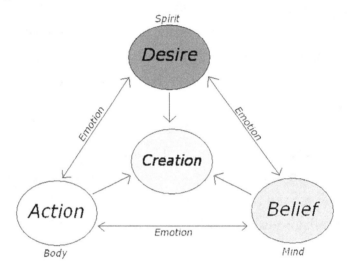

Figure 2. Abundance Model

In this book, we'll be working with the Abundance Model. This model shows us that the creation process can be tackled from multiple angles. For those of you who have been struggling with your "mindset" and trying to consistently visualize, you'll be relieved to learn that using your mind isn't the only way to manifest. Here, it allows you to create in multiple ways and also shows you a different perspective on what you need to do to keep yourself aligned with your natural state of Abundance.

The first thing you'll notice about this model is that it isn't linear, yet much of abundance teaching is linear in nature. We have been taught to visualize, create vision boards or hold a mental picture of what we want and that there is a simple sequence to manifesting.

While that may be true, it doesn't take into account that we are complex beings with all kinds of life experiences, history, conditioning, epigenetic programming, different energetic blueprints, karma, et cetera — often those personal things keep us from creating and effectively using a simple linear model.

We are also not all designed to create in the same way, nor do we have the same definition for success.

The Abundance Model shows us that our desires, beliefs and actions are all a part of creating. Emotional energy is the driving force of our creative power and the way in which we activate the creative process is unique to each and every one of us.

You're going to learn how your unique Human Design interfaces with the Abundance Model. By discovering who you are, how you operate and what you're here to do, you will also tap into your power to create a life that feels abundant and bountiful to you.

I hope that this information has given you a good start in realigning how you think and create. Understanding the mechanics of how you create and what has been influencing your choices until this point is an important part of transforming your capacity to truly tap into the abundance that is here for you.

As you've just read, just changing your mind or your thinking isn't always so easy. Most of us are hard-wired to have an open mind that is fluid. Just trying to consider things differently isn't usually enough to support making real change in your life.

What we see from Human Design is that we learn best when we understand information cognitively and when we are emotionally inspired by stories that deepen our engagement with new information.

The next section of this book is a collection of Human Design stories written to inspire you and help you see that you are not alone in the story of your own journey to abundance. It is our desire that you read these stories, finding pieces of your own story and inspiring you to keep discovering your own unique path to abundance.

It is also our intention that you find stories from people who have similar energy themes and Types as you. We want you to know that even though you are unique, you are also not alone.

Figure 3. Karen Curry Parker

Karen Curry Parker, B.S.N., C.P.C., is an international speaker and #1 bestselling author of *Understanding Human Design the New Science of Astrology: Discover Who You Really Are.* Karen has personally trained thousands of people to use Human Design helping them identify, resolve and overcome habits as well as conditioning that has kept them stuck.

Karen's work has been featured on Fox News, Bloomberg Businessweek, CBS, ABC and various radio shows and tele-summits. Karen, along with her husband, is the founder of Sustainability 2027, a nonprofit business incubator dedicated to supporting women entrepreneurs and small home-based businesses.

Some of Karen's books include *Understanding Human Design, the New Science of Astrology: Discover Who You Really Are, Inside the Body of God, 13 Strategies for Thriving in a New World* and *No Mistakes, How You Can Change Adversity into Abundance.*

# Section 1
# Life Patterns and Human Design

# Alana Heim

# Money

If I were to ask you to define wealth, how would you do it? Maybe it means a large sum of money or all of your worldly possessions? If you said something similar to either of these, you would be right on track with what a majority of people equate to wealth. I have worked in the financial industry for the past fifteen years as a Certified Public Accountant and a Certified Financial Planner™. The industry in which I work has us all believing that wealth is only about money. From my personal experience assisting clients with accounting, budgeting, taxation, financial planning, retirement planning and estate planning, I have seen them fearful and hateful of money. Those feelings cause angst within families, friends and beyond. For many people, this is their reality. Most believe there is no changing this reality. I strongly disagree.

For many years, I would work with clients who were all hurting from their relationship with money. Sometimes it had to do with their business. Even though it was doing well, the owners felt like they just couldn't earn enough. They would get upset about owing increased taxes, even though they had a tremendously successful year. I noticed quite easily the hang-ups surrounding their success. Either they were too afraid to fail (which caused them to limit themselves in their business practices) or they were too afraid to succeed (causing them to overwork themselves).

Other times, clients' loved ones would pass away, leaving them devastated. They would have no time to grieve because they were suddenly thrown into the administration of an estate where they knew nothing. Suddenly, beneficiaries were demanding a distribution from their executor sibling. They hadn't gotten along in twenty years, and now they were tied up in litigation for many more years to come. It was so disheartening to see time and again. If only their parents had planned differently for how their wealth would pass hands. If only my clients had been notified of their parents' estate planning and how that would affect them. If only...

I see the heartaches that each of us has felt with our relationship with money and wealth. We have all been led to believe that only a small percentage of the population is capable of achieving a wealthy status. We work harder and harder, and yet we still can't get ahead. We agonize about paying our bills and spending money. Most people do not hold a value for saving for the future or for retirement. Many even see value in spending exorbitantly through debt just to enjoy the façade of being wealthy, all while drowning inside and losing a part of their identity. The more debt, the harder the struggle. The more the anger takes over all thoughts, the deeper the emotions produce this downward spiral.

I started listening to podcasts and attending online seminars as well as summits looking for information that I could share with my clients to help their relationship with money. This is when I stumbled upon Human Design. The investigator inside me took over. I just had to know as much as possible. The light bulb didn't just turn on, it burst over my head.

Finding out that I am a Projector was like a sigh of relief. My inner guides had been calling to me, and I could finally hear them. The more I learned about myself, the more my life made sense. I finally understood why I was invisible more times than not and why my open Throat was never heard. I understood why I had been drawn to this path of guiding and assisting others. Knowing that I am emotionally defined helped out tremendously with understanding that I needed time to process decisions.

It was also a game changer. I could finally see that the path I had taken was one that I had been falsely conditioned to believe was my destiny. The reality is that it was a path that was draining the life out of me and burning me out — fast. I was sitting at a desk eight to nine hours per day, five days per week. Isn't that what society has us believe is the normal and only way of life? Well, I am not a Generator, and the stress was really taking a toll on my personal relationships and my livelihood. The past fifteen years of strenuous and grueling tax seasons were breaking me. My heart was telling me to follow my design and to follow my soul's path to prosperity through giving, serving and guiding. Nature was calling me to come out and play: to put my feet in the dirt and to feel the sun warm my skin.

Enter my dilemma. How could I guide others when I was stuck working at a desk for someone else? Even though I was building up a tremendous knowledge base and could offer the occasional nugget of wisdom to my clients, it wasn't on a deep enough level to fulfill me. I started to realize that I couldn't fully share my gift, and it was beginning to tear me apart. My limitations were crashing over me and I was drowning. I was feeling helpless, sad, unfulfilled and I did not completely understand why. I loved my family, my home and my community. And of course I loved my job, didn't I? Then why didn't it feel right anymore?

As I learned more about my own personal design, I could tell that a new future was on the horizon. I started to visualize where I wanted to be, the person I was becoming. What a beautiful thing to envision the new me and to fall in love with that person, that future. I began to create voids in my life that the universe could fill. I began visualizing myself as an entrepreneur and attending events that would give me the information necessary to get out on my own — as a guide. The more I visualized, the more I could feel my soul rejoicing and cheering for me. Everything that would normally be considered a scary process felt suspiciously calm. I felt an inner peace that I had never experienced. Here I was stepping out of my comfort zone only to find myself in a different one that was actually very natural.

Since finding Human Design, my values have exponentially evolved and taken priority within me. I no longer see wealth as just a large amount of money or possessions. I see that wealth applies to everything. I am wealthy in knowledge.

I am wealthy in the passion I have to effect change in the world by guiding others to embrace and heal their own wealth attributes as well as personal strategies. I am wealthy in freedom to do that which I desire. I am wealthy in the love I receive from my family, friends and nature. I am wealthy in love that I have to offer to everything I encounter. I am wealthy in the inner beauty I possess and graciously share with the universe.

Wealth does also encompass money, and money is whatever you choose it to be. Money is love. Money is beauty. Money is our friend. It loves us just as we love it. Money is energy. We are all energy, and together we can build a relationship with money that dances in harmony. The energy of money needs to flow. The more kind we are with embracing the flow of that energy, the kinder the universe is with us. When we give with pure intentions, the universe rewards us twice over or even tenfold. When we have excess wealth, it is up to us to see the beautiful choice that money has given us: to either continue accumulating or to effect change in the world by sharing it to make an impact greater than ourselves.

Look at your relationship with money, and decide if you see it as evil or as a loving resource that can be shared. It is possible that you desire money just so you can be happy, but you might see the greater potential that money can offer to others as well as yourself. Money is a resource, and some of us hold on to that resource too tightly while others of us throw it away as quickly as it is received.

When money sits stagnantly, the energy inside us does the same. The greed that could potentially be inside us continues to brew and create negative energy. But when we remove that resistance and follow our heart, joy springs forward and the flow of energy gushes graciously through us. When you unconsciously hold on to money because you are fearful that you may never receive it again, you also send negative vibrations out into the universe because you are focusing on the negative aspect of never receiving it again. Where you focus is what you attract.

We can bless our money and graciously invest it in ourselves, in our future, in a charitable organization, or in the lives of others who make an impact on us. What you value most is where you will likely give easily. What areas in your life cause you to struggle in being gracious with your spending? Perhaps you dislike paying rent — or maybe you are grateful to have a roof over your head in the interim until you are able to purchase a home. You could angrily pay for a broken windshield that some rock caused — or thank the windshield for serving and protecting you from harm. Every situation is a learning experience, and every experience can be handled negatively or positively. The choice is yours to make.

The choice is always there whether you are picking out your clothes, deciding what to eat for dinner or spending money where it calls you. And money does call us. When something is just too perfect, we act instinctively without hesitation. When something feels right, we just know how to respond. It is part of our design. When you do what feels right for you, you can never make a mistake. You can only do what is best for you. I urge you to embrace money in this fashion. Let it guide you to spend where it feels really good to you, and you actually dance with joy when you let it flow to where it desires. Feel the power of that loving energy. It really is delightful.

We all have the potential to acquire wealth, especially when following our design. Life becomes easier, and resources flow more easily. When you love you, you love everything around you. When your thoughts are joyful, your emotions are purely electric with love. When your emotions are highly positive, your vibrations are positive and that is when the true Law of Attraction formulates. You begin attracting more and more love and positive outcomes in your life because that is the energy you are putting out into the universe.

The spectacular gift of Human Design is that it allows you to understand your conscious and unconscious beings. Many times, people fail to truly understand the Law of Attraction because although they are consciously attracting, they neglect to focus unconsciously on the same behavior. When you can love and accept yourself for who you are, the power you possess naturally unfolds effortlessly. The goodness in your heart and the happiness beaming through your eyes sets your path. Anytime we can love ourselves, we allow others to love us. We are able to receive gifts that would otherwise go unnoticed. When love pours out of us, we are giving on such a higher vibrational level to everything and everyone around us.

Human Design takes you on a breathtaking journey into your soul, your heart, your mind, and your inner guiding systems. You get to find you, become you and love you. It is a journey we each should take. It is a journey all parents should take so they can understand themselves and their children. Children are the legacies we leave behind, so it is our duty to lead them appropriately to find their true inner passions. It is our obligation to teach the children of our future to love and respect themselves so that they can create a loving relationship with money that they can share with the world.

Now I ask you again to review how you define wealth. Your definition may have evolved or it could create new problems for you. You may see the possibilities of new solutions to the issues you may be encountering right now. My intention is only to encourage you to open your heart and mind to the endless possibilities of redefining how you view the money and wealth in your life. You can be a role model for your children by showing them that money is a loving energy to be shared with others. Living that way now leaves the best legacy for your family. You may feel a calling to view money in a new, bright, shining light. You may even feel compelled to revise your own Will and Trust or speak to your family about your intentions to do more with the resources and money you will leave behind.

I believe in Human Design and the impact it can make on each of us. Knowing our energy design can assist us in ways that we cannot even fathom. I believe that being in alignment with our true, authentic self creates unlimited opportunities. Life becomes an easier, more beautiful journey that truly is prosperous.

Figure 4. Alana Heim

Alana Heim is a Certified Public Accountant, a Personal Financial Specialist, a Certified Financial Planner™ and a Human Design Specialist. (Although she is not from Anaheim, her name sounds like she is — she lives in Reno.) Alana is the Prosperity Alignment Coach and the founder of Prosperity Alignment, Inc.

She proudly and boldly takes clients on a unique, transformative journey around the Prosperity Compass™, her signature system. Through the confines of the Compass, she bridges the vision of who they want to be in alignment with who they are through Human Design. She then intricately guides them through their own self-healing work that is necessary to rewire their brain and shifts their DNA to remove the fears as well as limiting beliefs that hold them back. This deep work prepares them to investigate and then conquer the inner wealth issues that were imprinted upon them. At the end of the journey, they emerge as the beautiful soul they have always been: full of love and light, generous, authentic, empowered and living life with a passion that emanates from them.

Her vision is to lead humanity through this process of finding inner prosperity. Alana is an advocate for solidarity, philanthropy, and sustainability. She is a two-motors Projector,and lives with her projector husband, their three children and two cats.

# Kristin Shorter

# Family

It was the winter of 2009 and my four-year marriage ended, finalized with a divorce decree. It was the worst year of my life and it was finally over. But something new had begun to stir in me. I was repeating my parent's footsteps by getting a divorce and I thought about how my children were going to be affected by this decision. While I knew it was better for them to not be around arguing, yelling and nasty insults, I also knew the effects that divorce has having experienced it first-hand.

I started with concern and then worry, which moved to stress and fear then grew into terror of having my family fall apart, hate me and having to spend half their life in therapy. I did not experience any of this when my parents divorced but my imagination went wild.

In order for me to get a divorce, it was mandated that I take a parenting class. It was interesting and for the first time, I realized I could learn how to be a better parent! Because I wasn't working both a full-time and part-time job to keep my family sheltered, I actually had time to read!

I started reading everything I could including Christian parenting books and non-Christian books, birth orders, astrological signs and basically anything that I could think of that would help me understand my kids, to teach them how to make decisions that were correct for them.

The funny thing is that when you're reading so many books from so many different perspectives, they begin to contradict each other. That was painful and confusing. I became even more frustrated and unclear about how to keep a cohesive family that cooperated and was harmonious.

At the same time as all this reading, I had just finished my training as a Defense Initiated Victim Outreach specialist through the University of Texas in Austin. I saw an email about how to be a better public speaker. Something inside my gut knew that I had to be there and I was soooo excited. I loved speaking in college and felt this would improve my speaking ability as well as remind me of some of the key speaking elements I'd forgotten.

When I looked at the price my heart sank, it was $5,000. Being a single mom of three (amazing) kids didn't leave much left over at the end of the month, not to mention I had just gotten divorced, moved and was in a major life transition. But I was optimistic because the training was in The Woodlands, Texas — about an hour away. I wouldn't have to pay airfare or hotel accommodations.

I hand wrote a letter to the woman leading the event and I called as well as emailed her every day. And every day I wrote, called and emailed, I got a little more vulnerable until eventually my letter sounded like, "I'm desperate and hopeless please let me attend your event and I'll volunteer or work for you to pay off the debt." The facilitator called me and told me she had gotten my letters and she wanted me to come as her guest. I cried for 30 minutes after we got off the phone; it was the first time I felt this overwhelming sense of hope. I knew I was supposed to be there and I was going to be there!

When I arrived, the first morning we got into the basics. Then she asked me for my birth information and ran a peculiar looking chart. It was my Human Design chart and it fascinated me. I asked her to run one for my kids and I was flabbergasted. It was very compelling because of the accuracy. After she explained it, I had this deep understanding of myself that helped me realize where I had gone wrong, why I had gone wrong and how to go right next time. I wanted this for my kids:

- I wanted this for them at a young age so that they didn't have to learn by making my mistakes.
- I wanted them to know that whenever they made a choice they would know, every time, if the choices they were making were correct for them.
- I wanted them to have the awareness of their choice.

After the conference ended I was gifted the Human Design program. It divides everyone up into five different Types and gives everyone a Strategy to interface with the world. Within a year, I was through the program and taking the Level 4 certification. Another program started: Human Design for Parenting! Of course, I took that and began learning how to use this with my kids, how to share the information and explain it to them at their level of development.

I attribute Human Design to helping me heal after my divorce. I was able to forgive myself and had information that could actually support as well as nurture my kids. What I love about Human Design is that it gave me a deep understanding of myself and a Strategy for making decisions. I know when I'm off my path and how to get back on without self-criticizing or confusion. It's pretty clear cut. I see my strengths and vulnerabilities; I have learned techniques to balance myself and move forward confidently.

In Human Design, I'm a Generator, which means I use my gut to make decisions. The gut is referred to as the Sacral and so when my kids ask me for something and I respond using my gut, if it's no, I say sorry, Sacral said no... And we laugh. I've taught them their own Strategy. We're a family that knows each other, has a deep understanding of each other, and has the freedom to express ourselves.

My children were one, two, and ten when I first learned about Human Design. Now they're eight, nine, and fifteen. To see how they interact with others is so beautiful and the freedom they exhibit when making choices for themselves is amazing. They're self-directed and confident kids. When you understand your child, you can then help them support themselves and become independent. Human Design gives you the awareness of what each child needs. Once you start enforcing their Strategy, everything becomes so natural and so effortless for parents because not only do children feel loved and supported, they are also more capable because they, too, understand their Strategy.

For instance, when my daughter (Angie) was in elementary school, the school zoning changed every year so she changed schools frequently. Every time she had to make new friends, had new teachers and had a new environment. A lot of the kids would tell her, "You're so weird," and she asked me what that meant. According to her Human Design, she is very individualistic. She lives outside the box so to speak. From a Human Design perspective, she also is designed to be "weird" if you will. After I divorced, we moved again but now I had her Human Design. I told her that when people are saying, "You're weird," what they're really saying is "Why aren't you conforming? Why aren't you being like the rest of us?" She needed to understand that when she's being "weird" she's actually giving others permission to be themselves.

She started playing basketball for the new school and initially the girls on the team sang the same song, "You're so weird." She'd come home and tell me what they said and I'd reiterate that she has to be herself, and people will come to love her. One time during basketball practice, one of the girls got mad at my daughter and started saying they wanted to fight her. Before my daughter could respond, three older girls all stood up for Angie telling the other girl that in order to fight my daughter, they'd have to fight them first. She's made lasting friendships that support and nurture her. She's being herself and accepts others who are also "weird."

One of my sons is a Projector. His Strategy is to be invited and he loves invitations. Knowing this, we frequently invite him to give us advice. He understands his energy needs and when he's ready to be alone will depart from playing outside with friends and stay in his room to play alone. The kids will periodically check on him by knocking on the door to see if he is ready to join them again. He's learned how to get invited. He has a strong propensity to doubt himself. I've been able to teach him how to channel the doubt into information. If someone says something that doesn't make sense and he believes them which turns into him getting duped, he struggles to find his bearings again. Now, with Human Design, we see that doubt is part of his design but it's not supposed to be directed toward the self. It's supposed to be directed toward information. Now he questions what people tell him (including me) in order to make choices that are correct and support him.

My other son is a Manifestor, and these are rare Types in Human Design. Since he was born he's been so independent. He would dress himself at a very early age and learned to walk by himself and ride a bike by himself, occasionally letting me help him. He would go off on his own and according to Human Design, this is correct for him. In order to feel connected to your child as a mom, you want to be able to care for them and receive care from them. He doesn't like affection or being held. He's usually hot, so snuggling with him was also uncomfortable. I struggled with how to feel loved and give him love the way I usually do. Knowing Human Design has helped me realize this trait isn't personal. When I want to be appreciated I tell him what he can do for me, such as opening my car door or restaurant doors, getting me drinks and simple things like that are more comfortable for him.

Having Human Design has helped me in so many ways, not just within my family. It's also taught me how important it is for me to exercise. After having three kids, I've put on a few pounds and the way I'm designed is to exhaust myself at the end of every day. I know what you're thinking: working and having three kids is exhausting! It is, but more than just mentally exhausting itself, my body needs to move. It is also an indicator for me when I'm off my path. Dancing is really good for me. Because I carry a lot of tension in my body getting regular massages is also good for me.

My sons are different; they don't need to exercise every day. They can actually go longer periods without exercise. However, sleep is a little more difficult. They need to be lying down before they get tired. It's hard enough getting them to lie down when they are tired — try doing it when they're not tired! When they do this, they get rejuvenating sleep; without it, they sleep but wake up still exhausted.

When it comes to finances our family is what my Mom refers to as "New Age." I allow my kids to earn a decent allowance. There are chores they have to do because they're a part of our family and after those chores are done, then they can earn money from doing other chores. The reason for this is because one, I was going to spend the money on them anyway so why not let them help out around the house and two, they need to learn about money now rather than later. When I was 18, I went on a fun shopping spree, and it went on for three years. I really understood money when I cut up my credit cards and began paying them off.

Hopefully, my kids won't have to learn that lesson because they're learning about it without being able to get a credit card! Just because the kids have this extra money that doesn't mean that they get to buy toys. In our family, they have to buy their own snacks (junk food). When we'd go out to eat, I'd usually buy them a milkshake which cost me about $3.00. When they began earning their own money, I told them to pay for half of the dessert if they wanted it. They quit ordering milkshakes because they didn't want to spend $1.50, but they had no problem with me spending $3.00! The lightbulb went off in my head: the money they earned needed to buy the things they needed and some things they wanted like toys and cool Minecraft shirts. When my kids want something they ask "Mom, how can I earn $10?" The house gets cleaned and they take better care of the toys they buy.

For my sons and me, it's important for us to have a foundation that includes a financial foundation. It provides a confidence and stability that feels secure. My daughter is a little different because she needs to be challenged with learning. She is in honors classes and still has a lot of time on her hands. I started challenging her to learn something new once a month and she could earn an extra $100.

Today, there are a lot of single moms that don't have the support they had in the past. Using Human Design to learn a tidbit that can help you save money and educate your children at the same time is going to save a lot of time and energy. I love helping others awaken to their own deep understanding of themselves and learning their Strategy through Human Design. They can then use that knowledge to help their children deeply know themselves and be better prepared throughout their life.

Figure 5. Kristin Shorter

Kristin Shorter first found Human Design in 2010 after getting her Bachelors in Psychology and working as a certified Victim Outreach Specialist with the University of Texas in Austin. She is a Certified Human Design Specialist Level Four as well as a Certified Family Coach offering Human Design Readings, Family Analysis, Sacral Sessions, Generator Coaching and Relationship Readings.

She loves sharing Human Design with people because of the evolution of clients truly understanding themselves and remembering their life purpose. Kristin works with clients all over the world, participating in speaking engagements, seminars and trainings.

This single mother of three brilliant children personally attests that Human Design is a powerful tool that can truly and profoundly change your world and that of your family.

# Quay Whitlock

# Vision

Many years ago, I worked for Alvin Ailey American Dance Theater. I would often hear a quote that Mr. Ailey was famous for saying: "Dance came from the people and it should be delivered back to the people." When I think about Human Design, I am reminded of that quote as I believe Human Design was created for people — for everyone, and it should be delivered to everyone.

I believe the excitement of discovering Human Design happened out of desperation. Prior to my introduction to Human Design, I was pretty depressed. My journey began a few years ago while sitting in my office unfulfilled and in need of change. I admit I was in a major funk that affected ALL areas of my life. I knew I wanted something radically different but I didn't know what it looked like... I had no clue.

Life Coaching was definitely not on my radar at the time. I remember trying to figure out ANYTHING in life that would bring me joy and happiness every day. The very first image that popped in my head kind of shocked me: I saw myself picking up my four-year-old daughter from school, walking hand-in-hand and chatting about her day. The image was so vivid. l really saw myself doing just that. I suddenly felt such joy as well as happiness at the thought of something so simple, and I knew I could not make that happen while sitting behind a desk working for someone else.

To help this come about, for several months I meditated, prayed, used creative visualization, participated in an incredible and intense leadership program, enrolled in various courses to support my new endeavor, hired my own coach and believed in the POSSIBILITY that I could create this beautiful life that I so desperately needed. That's when Human Design found me. I decided to focus on how I could help myself and during the process, I was inspired to help empower other women to achieve similar goals.

Fast forward to today when I am truly living that vision. I didn't know it at the time but I was actually following my Human Design Strategy. I am what is known as a Manifesting Generator. Our Strategy is to envision what we want. We "imagine first and visualize the outcome," inform others and then wait for the universe to bring it into reality so that we can respond.

I asked the person who introduced me to this incredible modality a few years ago how it was possible that Human Design had been around for more than 25 years, yet hardly anyone has ever heard of it. It's baffling to me that something so powerful can support e-v-e-r-y-b-o-d-y on the planet, but thus far only a small percentage of people know that it exists! When I tried to describe my initial human design session to my family and friends, I basically told them it felt like he (the consultant) has been attached to my hip since birth.

I recall asking something about how the consultant could possibly know the essence of who I am at my core when we just met; yet, he knew the way I mentally process things, my need to "keep busy," the depth of my intuitive nature, my ability for me to manifest things for myself and others. He simply replied, "Well, I'm no psychic, nor do I have much intuition, but the information is right here in your chart, your unique blueprint, and I'm just sharing it."

Well... *what could I say to that response,* I thought, with a grin on my face. That is when the excitement started to bubble. In that moment, unbeknownst to me, I had discovered my purpose and my mission in life. A few months later, I began my personal journey with studying Human Design.

Now, I feel called to share Human Design with the world: from a stage, in a book, at parties and gatherings, with clients old and new, shouting from the mountain tops with anyone and everyone who will listen. I realize this may sound a little like I am a genius to some people and a freak to others, but I don't care. Ironically the "genius/freak" perception is actually a part of my unique design, go figure!

While I consider myself to be a spiritual person (one who is a little "woo" but not necessarily "woo woo"), I realize that many people on the planet are neither. What does this mean for them? Can they not benefit from the amazingness of Human Design because they can't see beyond the trees to the "spiritual forest"? My soul feels deeply for the people who make up this part of mankind; it has become my mission to stand for them. I support them in looking beyond the information they must provide in order to gain access to unlocking the key to their brilliance, their true inner beauty, their sheer magnificence.and their life's purpose filled with passion. I want to help them view

Human Design as they would Myers-Briggs, Carl Jung's Archetypes, really any personal assessment tool so that they recognize the unique, individual, one of a kind blueprint that mirrors the unique, individual, one of a kind person they are.

What I love about Human Design is that it can be used to complement other modalities, tools and ideas that you may already be studying. It, too, can enhance your life. You do not have to choose to use Human Design as a replacement for what's been working for you, simply learn about your own unique decision-making Strategy so you can use that Strategy along with your preferred practices. Human Design is not an "either/or" concept. It is truly a "both/and" experience where you can have the best of both worlds and benefit tremendously. For example, you can take the principles of Napoleon Hill's "Think & Grow Rich" or any online course and marry them to your Human Design Strategy in order to obtain the best results possible for you.

I had imagined my family truly loving life and experiencing the opposite of the life we had been leading. I informed my husband of my desire and enrolled him in the vision as well. Together, we waited and watched as God and the universe revealed signs, synchronicities and opportunities for us to respond.

Within the year after starting this journey, we moved from New York City to sunny California for a better quality of life. We just packed up our family and created a joyous "work-life blend." Not only do I get to pick up my daughter from school and bond over the details of her day, but I am able to experience many things I love (including a daily prayer/meditation practice, walks along the beach, hiking, etc.). Along the way, I was also able to enjoy many more things: more quality time with family and friends, walking away from a six-figure salary with the confidence that I can (and will) create abundance doing what I love, begin to work with powerful dynamic women, volunteer more, renew my happiness, follow my curiosity and enjoy my bliss.

Human Design has truly transformed my life. Becoming a Human Design specialist, an Abundance by Design facilitator, and a Healing by Design specialist not only helped support me on my journey, but it has made me a better parent to my child and partner to my husband. I see them and understand them in a way that I didn't previously. For example, most (if not all) parents believe their child is talented in some way or another. The fact that my daughter has something called "The Talent Line" has given me the motivation to support all of her interests and allow her to pursue many endeavors without trying to shut her down, say that she is doing too much or that she must pick one thing. I now have an even stronger desire to give her the freedom to figure out not only where she is talented, but also where her passions lie. When I want to support my husband with his entrepreneurial pursuits, I remind him of specific things in his chart that show his brilliance. For example, he is able to see and forecast trends, something that comes naturally to him and is clearly outlined in his design.

As a child, I often wondered why I was able to "see" visions about people and situations that came to pass. I have an uncanny ability to intuitively know things. I have since learned through discovering my Human Design that my completely open Spleen supports this experience. It's also the reason why I haven't experienced much fear. That's not to say that I don't experience fear at all, but I now know the fear I do experience probably belongs to someone else so being in their company may amplify it for me. Just recognizing this possibility has supported me in a tremendous way. Instead of freaking out about a circumstance or situation that I may feel fear around, I now "pause" and ask myself if the feeling is really mine. More times than not, I realize the answer is usually no.

As a teen, I was keenly aware that people listened to me and loved to seek my advice about relationships, career choices, friendships and general things to support their best interests. They trusted that the answers I gave, knowing they would help them in some way. Learning that my design contains the Channel of Structuring has helped me understand how I am able to support others. The gift that I have been given is to provide insight, the ability to paint the bigger picture, this "third eye" quality that often blurts out "I know, I know" yet I can't quite explain "how" I actually know. Unfortunately, this same channel in its lowest expression is the probable cause for my daughter to also say to me, "Mommy, you aren't listening to me!" That statement breaks my heart, but I have learned to forgive myself and have taught her to "give Mommy a gentle touch when you feel I'm not paying attention." This is a solution I'm not sure I would have come up with had it not been for the guidance I've received with understanding my design.

There are other ways I see my Profile coming through in my life, too. As a young adult, I marveled at my attitude around money, with an inner knowing that I could always figure out a way to create abundance or that God would always provide for me financially. In college when I temporarily worried that I wouldn't have the funds to pay my bills, out of the blue a job opportunity would appear or an unexpected check in the mail. This and so much more was reflected back to me when I was given my Human Design blueprint. My chart includes the Channel of the Alchemist (the definition of an alchemist is having the ability to turn base metals into gold). I smile whenever I think about this because the book "The Alchemist" by Paolo Coelho is one of my top three all-time favorite books.

The messages in The Alchemist are similar to the saying "give me lemons and I'll make lemonade" or a coach telling you to figure it out for yourself. If you give me something that's a struggle, I'm going to figure out how to make it shine. Lately, I find myself in conversation with quite a few friends who are suddenly at a crossroads with their careers and experiencing a bit of what I experienced a few years ago. Because I've had the great fortune of knowing how amazing they are at their craft, together we have been able to come up with ideas to turn their years of experience into new and exciting paths, usually the road to being an entrepreneur.

My design also includes the Channel of Money (otherwise known as The Money Line). Although it does not necessarily mean I will become a billionaire in this lifetime (although a girl can dream), it does mean that I have an immense capacity to make money, to be comfortable in the material world, to manage things and create an abundance of resources for all. I once read that I share this same channel with actress Angelina Jolie, which is an example worthy of repeating. Not only does she have a significant amount of wealth, but she is also an inspiring ambassador of goodwill though her appointment by the United Nations.

When I think about being in the company of other people, I am usually rolling up my sleeves ready to pitch in and offering to help. My friends can attest that I've pretty much always been that way. I just want to help people live their best life with ease. If I can help make that possible with a hug, volunteering or a strategy session, for example, I'm most likely going to do it. Having the Gate of Contribution in Human Design has helped me understand my need to make a contribution, my desire to be a philanthropist and my goal to inspire and create change for mankind.

I share these things not to simply point out some of the specifics of my Human Design, but the importance of showing how you too can connect the dots, how you can reflect on the things you've experienced, how you can tie them to who you are at your core, to truly understand your way of being and to accept the beauty of how and why you were created. Simply put, Human Design helps you to be the best version of you, uniquely you, and to share your gifts with the world as well as the people in it who are waiting for you.

I am so excited to be on this path of living my purpose and sharing my gifts with the world. I truly believe I am here to connect, inspire and transform lives while working with change-makers who are also on a mission to make this world a better place. And I love sharing Human Design in my own simple way, usually relating it directly to my clients' lives and helping them become their best self. I listen to their pains and struggles that are blocking their path to their purpose. But the most joyous part is to witness the "light bulb moment" when they "get it" as something stands out to them and they experience the shift. Those moments are so inspiring to me, so magical and sacred that I feel incredibly blessed and honored their soul has chosen me to join them on their journey, to be one of their biggest cheerleaders and to witness their transformation.

Recently, that happened while I was on a live chat for a Human Design class I am taking. We were discussing a part of the chart called the Incarnation Cross. It has been described as the "cornerstone to your life purpose" and an "authentic illumination to one's life path." There are 192 Incarnation Crosses and I learned that it makes up about 70% of the personality characteristics we are here to express in life (our Design).

When looking at my overall chart and referencing my "cross" (Incarnation Cross of Contagion), the following was shared about me:

"Through your dedication and commitment and the intensity of your desire and passion, you are able to make a difference in the world by helping people reconnect to their abundance and you are here to share with great power and fire the information that is coming through you with the world. You are here to teach, share and set people on fire with new ideas."

I love this description because when I think about helping people "reconnect to their abundance," I am committed to helping them experience and live abundantly in all areas of their lives, not just financially, but in also in their relationships, in their desires, in their purpose and more. In my opinion, there is always room to experience more abundance even when life is fantastic.

It reminds me of an experience I had with a client. Our intention around coaching and exploring Human Design was initially for her new endeavor as an entrepreneur. However, the conversation led to her sharing about her husband and how many people come to them seeking relationship guidance because they've had a very successful and happy marriage for more than 25 years. She also shared that their friends and family don't offer them "relationship advice" because they assume they have it all. When I inquired if she would like to understand her husband's

Human Design and the composite design they create together, she quickly became intrigued.

Through Human Design, I was able to confirm personality traits that she had experienced over the years. By interpreting both of their charts, we were able to explore who they are as individuals and what magical energy they create when they are together. Then utilizing the intuitive energy present in my own chart, I was able to connect with her energy and gently but firmly guide her into seeing the powerful being that she was created to be. Our unplanned relationship coaching reframed her way of seeing how her husband's gifts compliment her own gifts and how together they can deliberately experience more joy and abundance.

If you are seeking the next chapter in your life, one that will bring you more passion and joy, one that makes you feel inspired to begin each day and is filled with doing more of the things you love, then I invite you to connect with a Human Design practitioner. Our goal is to support you, help guide you to living your purpose and create a beautiful abundant life.

Figure 6. Quay Whitlock

Human Design "found" Quay R. Whitlock during a dark and challenging time in her life. At a moment when she should have been feeling blessed to have found love after 40 and giving birth in her 40's, she felt rushed, depressed, frustrated and questioned her life's purpose. She desperately wanted the freedom to spend more quality time with her family, yet her current circumstance had prevented her from living the life she desired.

After leaving "corporate America," Quay has been studying Human Design for several years with a focus on both Healing by Design and Abundance by Design. She feels truly blessed and grateful for being introduced to this one-of-a-kind modality. Her most recent and significant contribution is her work as an Abundance by Design Facilitator. Quay also developed an online series of Abundance by Design group coaching programs focused on helping people live their best and most magnificent life, full of abundance, passion and joy.

Quay and her family currently live in Los Angeles, California, where they enjoy daily sunshine, walks on the beach, community and a life they curated by using their unique Human Designs.

# Linda Grace Farley

# Accomplishment

Imagine, having all the answers available to you in the palm of your hand. A roadmap that guides you through all the intricate pathways of life, one that centers you, enhancing your power of free will to make your own decisions. A roadmap that would not only take away all the uncertainty but also be the safe harbor to assist you in handling any life challenges. If this was available to you, would you partake in this excursion? I did and that's the day my life began, the day I discovered Human Design.

But first, so the journey is from the beginning: I was raised in an Italian Catholic environment. My dad (Italian) was a spiritual individual, interested in esoteric subjects, including natural medicine, while my mom (Irish/German) was conditioned by modern society to follow traditional medicine. It was interesting to witness the difference between their beliefs. As their daughter, I carried on the legacy of both but was pulled toward my dad's way of thinking.

In primary school, I was drawn to Astronomy, which led me into Astrology and Hinduism. I was fascinated by these topics but good teachers were hard to find back in the late 60's. When graduating from high school, I wanted to be an accountant; I was a natural. I loved the organization of it — recording or manipulating numbers, the completion of the process. Unfortunately, I could not afford college tuition, so I jumped immediately into the workforce. I trained to be a certified nurse's aide, working at one of the local nursing homes, but after about six months I became disheartened by what I witnessed. It seemed people were just discarded, thrown into an institutional environment to finish up their remaining years without impact to their families.

Inside the facilities, they weren't treated any better either. Their lack of empathy, lack of respect, lack of patience was too overwhelming for me to handle. I could not sit by and watch this day after day how these people suffered. I walked away from that field and went into the computer industry because I didn't have to feel, all I had to do was use my logic mind and physical body.

This field fit well with the things I liked about accounting. I still had the goal to be a Subject Matter Expert on mainframe computers. As the years went by, I increased my knowledge and learned how to connect, to think like the computer operated. One day, I discovered an aspect of computers that involved the impact from outside energy. The concept was exciting as well as rewarding since it led me to opening yet another field to explore: energy medicine.

Energy Medicine looks at how we all possess certain abilities and what opportunities were available to become an energy healer. Since that time, I have acquired different modalities, which expanded my appreciation and knowledge of this wonderful field. The course in Light Body Medicine with Dr. Alberto Villoldo was no doubt one of the best programs I experienced. This program woke me up. It brought me back to appreciating Mother Earth, sacred passages and understanding the undeniable Divine Force that exists in everyone and everything. While studying the subject, I changed perspectives somewhat back to some aspects of the nursing assistant and wanting to be of service to others. To my surprise, I found myself assisting loved ones in walking away from the ledge, to picking themselves up after one of their loved ones abandoned them and assisting them in opening their eyes to a different way of life, to realizing their potential. This evolved into life coaching.

I researched various organizations and actually completed an online certification. I became a member of coaching communities, increased my awareness and expertise in how to be one of the best coaches available. I have known quite a few people who have paid an enormous amount of money to enlighten themselves and they're still not fulfilled, not satisfied. What people don't realize is that unless you do the "homework" with your own investigation, look at yourself in the mirror and commit to correct the situation, you will continue to wander aimlessly in search of the elusive "Holy Grail" while just getting more frustrated.

As I walked through Energy Medicine, I was introduced to the Human Design program in January 2014, a day etched in my memory forever. As I listened intently to the speaker discussing Human Design, her words resonated into the very depth of my core. My first thought was, "How brilliant!" I wanted to know more. When the interview was completed, a package was offered containing Level 1 and 2 training in Human Design plus a 30-minute reading. I jumped at the opportunity, sensing this was exactly why I had been searching and I have not looked back ever since.

I always search with the intention to connect the dots: who I am, why I am here, what is my mission and how I can improve? Rather than only a nugget, Human Design had the potential to provide me with a life-changing insight. The readings she shared would expose crucial details. When I had my personal session I was asked the broad question about focus for the session and I chose about health and my career.

At that time, I was approaching the third stage of my life (or as Jane Fonda has stated, "The 3rd Act"). I wanted this chapter of my life to be the stage that gave back, as in passing my wand of experience and knowledge to the next generation. My intention was to be a vibrant part of society until the day when I take my last breathe, and then I knew I would be satisfied with no regrets. Questions (among others) that needed to be answered: Was public speaking correct for me? Would I be strong and healthy enough to carry out my plan?

After reviewing my chart, some key personal health areas were immediately identified that I could have challenges with if I didn't pay attention to them. That in itself altered the way I live my life. She needed me to then focus more precisely on what I wanted for a new career and my immediate response was if I should enter the field of public speaking, something that drew my interest for some time. She looked at my chart and replied, "If you choose to go into public speaking, you would be very successful — that's your Strategy". One of her key points she explained to me was if I should choose to get into public speaking, I have the capacity to touch the hearts of my audience in a very deep way. Why? Because when they look at me they won't see me, but rather they will see themselves through me. My search was over! I've finally validated my existence.

Two months later and armed with a new sense of direction, I joined a chapter of the Toastmasters International club. I wanted to fine tune my skills to be a better speaker. I found speaking, creating topics and telling my story both easy as well as rewarding. Once I started, I didn't want to stop. I was thirsty for more. I wanted to experience all that Toastmasters had to offer — and wanted to reach the Distinguished Toastmasters title. I'm very happy to say I have successfully completed that goal, satisfying all Communication & Leadership requirements.

While completing these levels, I also wanted to connect to the Non-Profit sector. I discovered the more involved I am, the more energized I become. As a result of following my chart-mapped "plan" (Strategy), I'm starting to be recognized for my leadership abilities, my expertise and my communication skills.

I am a storyteller and I tend to use analogies to make my point. When discussing the opportunity for human growth, I ask, "Have you ever seen a plant that appears to be dying? What happens when you give it water and sun? Doesn't it start to blossom again?" I think this is similar to the human psyche. If you give a person what they so desperately need, they will develop into a most beautiful, exquisite being. I truly believe that's what Human Design has the capacity to provide to people. My accomplishments in such a short period of time are nothing short of amazing and I know there are opportunities continue.

Through these experiences, I have realized the true power of this program. All I did was follow my Strategy. I have made tremendous strides in living this "new" life in such a short period of time. My self-esteem has blossomed! I'm more confident; I'm a better communicator; I'm more empathetic and compassionate toward others. I'm able to articulate ideas to people and manage to provide them with inspiration to start thinking about things differently where they may not have done that before. This integrates nicely into my coaching practice. A Human Design reading provides the foundation, weekly assistance in living our Strategy — and coaching for me satisfies the human factor of listening, hugging and understanding.

In my Human Design Profile (Martyr / Heretic), I've been able to experience and differentiate whether or not an experience is something that I should ignore or pursue. When I consider my Human Design Profile, knowing I have the martyr traits means I need to experience life and that's what I have done. I noticed when I listened intuitively, I found rewarding paths that actually led to my emotional and spiritual growth.

Through all of the offerings, there are a chosen few and I believe the Human Design to be one beautiful example of this: that provides a tremendous amount of knowledge, which hits the core and provides direction to stop the endless searching. Human Design provides peace of mind and a higher level of enlightenment. For the first time in my entire life (61 years) there is a feeling of accomplishment as well as a feeling of satisfaction, of direction. I've never experienced before.

Everyone has a mission, and Human Design helps identify it in each of us. Could it be that its mission is to provide individuals with the capacity to see; to wake up from the illusion they call life? What makes everyone unique is their astrological alignment at that time of birth, indicated by an Astrology chart. Those degrees in that specific time, longitude and latitude are further enhanced into an even finer picture by a Human Design Profile that includes channels, lines, motor centers, etc. That expansion into an initial image illustrates their true signature, their true identity, that what makes them unique.

I believe that the potential everyone has, illustrated through their complete Human Design chart, would show how we all can succeed by following their Strategy. That's pretty awesome in my eyes!

Take a look at the world. We stand witness to how many people are hurting and feel hopeless. This is expressed in the many bankruptcies, drug abuse, divorces, failed businesses and displays of destruction throughout the infrastructure of our society. But if they were aware of their Strategy, do you think our environment would be different? I do. Society has been conditioned to believe and act a certain way and it doesn't have to be that way. For example: Let's say you became an executive assistant because your guidance counselor directed you to that profession based on the shortage in that industry plus the salary was appealing but in your Strategy working a 9-5 job is not your protocol. Do you think they're going to be happy? I would suspect not. Your life will be filled with resentment, detachment, frustration — which will ultimately impact both your professional life and those you're assigned to and your personal life.

John Lennon's song, Imagine, says "Imagine all the people, living life in Peace." I think the awareness of Human Design has the capacity to manifest this reality. It can happen by starting at birth when a child's chart is completed. Parents would be aware of the characteristics that make up their child's Strategy and be able to orchestrate activities for the child based on the baby's specific "plan" - their Strategy, giving them the ability to pave the way for their growth and success in the world. In turn, parents would understand themselves better because they would be keenly aware of any challenges they may encounter with this child. Could you imagine the possibilities for all future generations? Assisting children in realizing their true potential through Human Design, what a wonderful service that would be! A child who is aware or discovers early in their life's their mission by following their Strategy, wouldn't that do wonders for our global society. With more awareness, humanity would continue to morph into a higher level of consciousness. Even if they chose to travel down a different path for a short time, eventually these children would be more focused on bringing humanity back from all those years of aimless wandering. In returning to the collective consciousness, it would be an amazing time to be alive.

If everyone could experience a Reading, they would see that there are lines and channels that give you an in-depth look at your specific chart. When I get Human Design transit reports from a Human Design teacher (those weekly "keep on track messages"), I review my Chart and I am able to ascertain whether or not I'm going to be challenged this week!

Those messages about my own Human Design plan can be thought of like a ship on the ocean. A captain receives information from the Coast Guard that a storm is coming. The captain makes decisions based on that information. It's the same thing with Human Design transits. Once you're aware storms or wonderful opportunities are coming, you'll have a better understanding of how to maneuverer your life in all aspects: physically, mentally or spiritually. The transit's awareness assist me in making better decisions; as a result, I'm handling life a lot easier than ever before.

I said I'm a storyteller, so here's another example. It's like when playing the card game "Texas Hold 'Em." You need to know when to hold them and when to fold them. This takes practice. When you're aware of the energetic impact of the transits and you understand how these align with your Strategy, you can make those conscious decisions to obtain the best outcome. Even today with my admitted limited awareness of my Human Design program (since I've only been involved in it for two years, but it's changed my life), I am keenly aware at a deeper level than ever before. I increase my sensitivity through learning about this program, which then allows me to take or not take action at the most appropriate time for me.

My Human Design Profile is Martyr / Heretic, but my Strategy is a Manifesting Generator. My crown and heart are open. Because of this, I have this unique ability to brainstorm ideas and sometimes it feels almost like a feeding frenzy. If someone mentions something in a conversation and it clicks, I have the ability to kick off from their idea and grow it into another one all because I have these open Centers. I'm like a sieve where I have the ability to bring an idea in, manipulate it and produce another result. It's all because of these open Centers. The challenge for me is not immediately responding, and that's my protocol (how I am designed) — I need to be conscious of the invitation in order to proceed. In other words, I need an invitation to respond.

And that's another thing with Human Design. I'm keenly aware now if my mood changes when I'm around someone else. If I'm in a pretty good mood and I start having negative thoughts, I know that I've tapped into someone else's energy. I stop, take an assessment, tap into my body and ask myself the question "Is this mine?" If I come out of the process with a "No" response, I consciously release it. If

I receive a "Yes" response, then I address it accordingly and the same thing happens — I release it. That's the beauty of Human Design, no more second guessing.

By using the processes and levels in Human Design, I now have a way of understanding myself deeper. I'm consciously looking at my whole being. It's the depth of the program. After all, it's not as simple as just your astrological chart. When you pull in all these beautiful aspects of Quantum Physics, I Ching, Hindu chakra system plus Astrology, the depth of the outcome about the particulars specifically for you is tremendous. We, as human beings, are more powerful than we understand. But we don't have the tools to use our talents because we have not been given a map. With the information provided through the Human Design Chart, we now have the ability to evolve and to grow into more conscious empowered Human Beings, free from fear.

Human Design gives us the motivation to continue to move forward, but getting past our fears may be a bit more challenging. To help speed people along on their own journey (since that's one of the things that is in my Profile), I would recommend two exercises that worked wonders for me — and they aren't typically considered by people as a Human Design prospect. The first one came from the Seven Habits of Highly Successful people. Document all of the roles you play in life. Then imagine how you would want people to remember you once you left this Earth. That was an eye-opener for me. As I wrote down my answers, I woke up. I didn't want to be remembered in such a negative way. That was the start of my journey 30+ years ago.

The other technique I learned while studying Shamanism 12 years ago, and again it was before my Human Design learnings but it absolutely applies. The task is to write down all of your roles that you held in your life, both past and present. This time, reflect on each role, give thanks for the experience, release it and then place the paper that contained the name in a fire - thus burning your roles. That exercise in itself was tremendous. What I discovered was we haven't a clue how much energy is attached to those roles but once you've experienced this exercise, the sense of physical and emotional release is very much noticeable.

Both exercises are beautiful in so many ways, but they really are the lessons you learn in Human Design. And I'm still learning. My next step is to learn through Human Design classes the ability to interact more effectively with others, how to identify with others based on their strategy. We're all intertwined by various factors so why not seek to understand another better to produce a higher more evolved outcome?

Human Design has helped me to recognize my own vibrational aspect. It's actually assisted me in achieving that higher level of consciousness and understanding so that I can become more focused on accomplishing my mission. I can discern things better, and realize how deep the intensity of the human design strategy is or can be. It has the capacity to enable individuals to journey far beyond a normal surface perspective. The day I pulled my first chart, I was shown how philosophical and creative I can be. I am now very aware of why I have this wonderful capacity and use it to engage in creative brainstorming, where it brings the whole experience to a different set of outcomes, with a different perspective that I would have never encountered otherwise.

There aren't any restrictions; everything is only enhanced by all these other factors. It leaves me breathless and questioning how deep in thought do I have the ability to go? I actually ask that when I coach people. "How far down the rabbit hole do you want to go?" This is not a passing fancy that you just want to brush off dust when the time gets rough or uncomfortable. It takes commitment and you have to want this more than life itself. In order to be free, you have to be stripped bare, expose all you hidden thoughts, past hurt and look at yourself in the mirror. There you can determine whether you like the person you are — or not. If you don't like the person you are today, you have the ability to change it.

That's one of the most important messages when I reflect on the impact Human Design has made on me personally. I could have continued waffling around, being pulled in so many different directions. I was learning and being a temporary "subject matter expert" but not sure what the end result would be, if I would ending up walking down another path or still be thirsting for the answer. Before engaging in Human Design, I wanted closure, freedom and truth.

Wasting precious time and money is more visible when you get into the last cycle of your life. The days of being bombarded by all those quick fixes, all those too good to be true schemes are over. I now possess this knowledge, which gives me the ability to become more focused. I'm more focused now than I have been in any time in my entire life because I have discovered my mission, my strategy. I think if people really discovered their energetic design themselves (like so many of us who have discovered Human Design), there could be great positive impact on the world. I want to be one of those individuals, through public speaking and coaching, to assist individuals in their pursuit of their "Holy Grail" through finding their specific Human Design strategy. By telling my story of discovery, perhaps someone will take away that golden nugget of information and make the necessary steps toward a personal journey of discovery.

You know, there's a story I've seen on the internet about this little boy walking on the beach and he discovers hundreds of starfish beached all over the place. He immediately starts picking them up, throwing them back into the ocean. A gentleman witnesses his act of kindness and approaches him asking, 'What are you doing?' The boy replies, 'I'm saving this starfish.' The man says, 'But there's so many of them, you'll never save them all!' The little boy didn't say anything, just bent down picked up the starfish and through it back into the water. Then he stated, "I saved that one."

I keep that story in my mind every time I hear negative comments such as, "Oh, Linda, why get involved? You can't save that person." My answer is like the little boy's. I think everybody has the ability to be saved. I think everybody has the ability to wake up. That is my mission. Through my words, through being that communicator to be a coach and using my skills as an energy healer, I can assist in someone's journey to discovery. I've already had numerous examples of the gifts that I possess positively impacting other people and I don't take that lightly. The one that I hold most dear to my heart is the one that involved my dad.

Three months before his death, I went to visit my dad. He was sitting in his lounge chair and I could tell he was deep in thought. I asked him, "What's up, Dad? What are you thinking?" He had negative thoughts wandering in his head, and told me that he had so much regret. I said asked him why. When he explained it, he felt that he had missed so many opportunities because he allowed fear to control his life. I asked him if he was aware of a Chinese philosophy that states you measure your success in life by the success of others; I asked him to look at his life, his six beautiful children. Each one of us is very successful. Each one of us has children who are very successful. How can you deny that? He looked at me and stated that he never thought of it that way. I asked him if he was aware of the root of his problem. I explained that he always gave so much of himself but he never allowed anyone to love him. He said he never allowed it because he didn't think he was worthy of it.

Imagine 97 years of not knowing how to accept love. Imagine being close to your time ending on earth and so filled with regret that you're unable to appreciate and enjoy your last days on earth. My dad was not unique; there are many walking this earth with the same feelings. But my dad was one of the lucky ones because he had someone who loved him unconditionally and was willing to take the chance to help him tackle his demons before he embarked on his greatest journey. I was with my dad the day he transitioned. I'm convinced he patiently waited for me to return to his room as a sign of love and appreciation for opening up his eyes and helping him to see before he finished this part of the journey.

I understand why these types of experiences happen now. By having my chart read, it has reaffirmed my mission, has given me the strength as well as courage to speak to others, to touch them emotionally and spiritually and to touch their hearts. The sense of gratitude and appreciation reciprocated back to me is immeasurable. And that's another reason why I continue to learn more about my strategy of Human Design, so I can help even more people.

Just as with any subject, when you look for information on a topic you will find many resources. There are many instructors in Human Design. I have seen some of them and how they approach it through their YouTube videos, but there was something about the personal approach of the teacher I chose that attracted me, helped me to see clearly and have confidence that I was making the right decision. They say the moment the student is ready that the teacher will appear. In that fateful lecture, I just knew I had to learn more about Human Design and I had to learn it from *that* speaker. She understands at a much deeper level perhaps because of her experience. Her story, I totally understand. I've walked my own path, but I recognize some of her experiences and know that story all too well. I related some of that to her and perhaps that's why I feel comfortable and trust her, because of our shared background in experiences.

When you trust someone like that, then you're going to be more open to learning because you know that they're not going to give you false information or hope. The world is filled with individuals who will try to convince you that they can cure what ails you. They may have their titles, degrees and certificates, hanging their shingle saying how great they are or what they can do for you. But that is all a façade. When you're genuine, people just know; they can see past the façade and feel your honesty. That's what I found in my teacher and her approach to Human Design. That's what I hope all my clients will also see in me.

Before Human Design, I had a concept rolling around in my mind to develop a program and call it the Center for the Healing Arts. My friend (who has had extensive training as an Astro/Numerologist) and I discussed at length the footprint for this Center. We shared the belief that if people were actually shown their life blueprint, what made them unique via their astrological charts, they would be awakened and grow from the experience. That would be our foundation. We would be able to assist them in releasing whatever bound them energetically. She would read their astrological charts and I would do Energy Healing or coaching. But once Human Design came into the picture, I knew in my heart that this was the foundation required. Interesting enough, my friend couldn't grasp the concept because she had been so programmed in just the astrology and neurology aspect.

One day during one of our discussions, I mentioned how much I was learning with Human Design. I wanted to share it with her. I knew once she grasped it, she would be as intrigued as I am. I am keenly aware that she's a very visual person and decided to use this approach. I pulled her Human Design chart along with her brother's and her nephews'. I offered, "Let's take a look at your chart and then we'll look at your brother's and his children." I asked her if she saw the continuity, the patterns. "Do you see how each of you is complementing each other? Here, you have a channel that has unconscious energy but the upper part is undefined, but then you look at your brother's and his is defined! Do you see how powerful this is? You are in the nucleus of your family and you're able to accomplish things with ease because each one of you complements each other and you're stronger as a whole."

That's when she realized and understood. The excitement in her eyes explained it all, like a lightbulb going off in her brain. She sat in awe of what was in front of her. "Oh my God, Linda." When you're involving Quantum Physics, the I Ching, the Hindu chakra system and Astrology, it is so powerful. Of course, this has all been blended together for me since I've been trained and am very aware of the Chakra system as part of my Energy Medicine education (and I've had the End of Life Doula training). There's some serious stuff right here. I no longer find it necessary to search to connect the dots because right here, right now all that I seek is front of me. That to me is pretty awesome.

If I was to narrow it down to one thing, the little golden nugget of information to share with someone to get them interested and believing in how Human Design can improve life, it all it takes is to start that journey to discovery. If you commit yourself, the world will gladly present a whole different perspective to you and the universe works exquisitely on your behalf. Life doesn't get any better than that.

Yes, the rest of my life has begun. As Dorothy in the Wizard of Oz, I'm happily skipping down that magical yellow brick road of Life, that proverbial golden path. I find myself arm in arm with all my archetypes: The Lion, the Straw Man and the Tin Man. This reality — my life's journey — was confirmed that wonderful day of my reading in March of 2014, the day I discovered Human Design and my Profile, my Strategy.

Now, when I wake up in the morning with a renewed sense of gratitude, I look forward to wherever this wonderful life will take me. What exciting encounters will I experience today and every day! Maybe that's how we all can start. Care to join me? It's just a reading away.

Figure 7. Linda Grace Farley

Linda Grace Farley started her pursuit of "Mind/Body/Spirit connection" in 1986 after experiencing a health crisis that prompted her to evaluate options outside the western medical field. She embarked on a journey into holistic and esoteric realms, studying with Mind/Body/Spirit thought leaders such as Dr. Deepak Chopra, Dr. Greg Braden and Dr. David Hawkins.

Her business, Cycles of Life Management Services, focuses on coaching and healing modalities. After discovering the Human Design program, Linda incorporated this system into her practice. Her certifications include Human Design Certified Practitioner Level Four, Reiki Master (Usui), Light Body Medicine practitioner/ End of Life Doula through Four Winds and Dr. Alberto Villaldo, Past Life Regression Therapy (where she studied under Dr. Brian Weiss) and Conversational Intelligence™.

Linda, a member of Toastmasters International, is working on her Distinguished Toastmasters title which is an expression of her talents in leadership and communications. As a Toastmaster, she volunteers her time in conducting communication workshops in area schools. She also leads workshops, lectures and provides individual coaching, assisting her clients in realizing their true potential.

# Section 2
# Escape to Abundance with Human Design

# Tina Forsyth

# Pay Attention

"No."

Without even thinking, this was the first word out of my mouth when he proposed to me that day on the ski mountain. It was my gut response.

Then my brain kicked in, and I started thinking, *"Tina, you've already talked about getting married. Of course, you need to say Yes... You are already living together, so you may as well be married... You helped picked out the ring - how can you say no?"*

Despite what my gut was telling me, I thought about it; I turned my "No" into a "Yes" and was married within nine months.

From the outside, my marriage was fine. Truth be told, even from within it seemed like we should be happy together. But we weren't. Things weren't horrible in any traditional sense, but I always felt that something was off, that something was missing. I swept that under the rug and kept telling myself it was fine. I was being too picky; I should be happy with what I have. He's not mean or screwing around, so why should I complain?

I felt like a fraud and didn't know what to do about it. We were both quietly becoming more miserable, but we had two girls. There was no logical reason to end our marriage because that felt like a very irresponsible and selfish move (and I was raised to be neither of those things).

Then in December 2012, I did a Human Design reading with a Human Design specialist. One of the first things we discussed was that my gut is my decision-making Authority.

"Tina," I remember him saying, "Your gut always knows the answer, but anytime you let your head get in the way, that's where you get off track."

It was a lightbulb moment for me — right there, I could see every instance where listening to my gut had served me and where NOT listening to my gut had caused problems. My marriage, of course, was one of those latter instances.

I felt like I was validated:

- I WASN'T crazy, selfish, or irresponsible.
- My deep knowing that "something was off" was true.
- Sweeping "it" under the rug was the irresponsible move.
- I am wired to follow my gut, and it will always serve me when I do.

My husband and I split up six months later. It was only after our separation that he revealed to me the truth: he was a transgender woman trapped in a man's body. My gut knew all along, and once I started paying attention, we were both set free.

Human Design has changed my life more so than any other assessment I've done (I'm an assessment junkie and have done many). Not only did it solve the dilemma of my marriage, it has become a huge asset to my business as well.

I've had my company since 1999, and my business has evolved from being a 1-1 service-based business to a successful training and coaching company.

For the first 10 years, I "went with the flow" and simply followed what life offered to me. It was great, and not only did it get me to six-figures, it also allowed me to create a business where I work part-time hours while raising my girls (who are now eight and ten years old.)

A few years back, I started feeling like I "should" be growing more. I could see the success that others were creating and felt like I had to do the same. I started building on other people's models and following the "formulas" they used to create success, because that's what I'm supposed to do, right? Regardless of what was tried, I always felt like I was pushing a string uphill. Yes, I would make a bit of progress, but it always ended up feeling empty, so I would turn to the next thing and keep trying.

I started to question my success:

- Why does this stuff seem to work for everyone else but not me?
- Am I cut out for this?
- What's wrong with me?
- What am I missing?

When I learned my Human Design, I was able to see WHY things weren't working the way I thought they should. Most notably for my business was learning that I'm a Generator, not a Manifestor.

When I first learned this, I will admit I was kind of annoyed! *"I MUST be a Manifestor,"* I thought. *"I like to take charge and make stuff happen. Look at all that I've accomplished so far. How could that possibly happen without being a Manifestor?"*

But then when I thought about it, I could see that what had been so frustrating in my business for years was I was trying to initiate. I would push to do what I thought I was supposed to be doing to create success. Every step felt like three steps forward and two steps back. Even when progress was being made, it never felt satisfying and always felt really hard. True success for me - the moments that have been the most fulfilling - have been the ones where I've been working in response to others or to a situation where I've paid attention to my gut.

As Generators, we are workhorses and can get stuff done, though we need to do work we LOVE or we will suffer for it. I'm almost embarrassed to admit how many seemingly successful aspects of my business — areas that make me money — are actually built around stuff that I don't enjoy. How often I've said yes to a project or a client simply because they asked something of me and I ended up hating the work. How many times I've sacrificed what I want to keep others happy. (Ouch!)

Knowing that I CAN do something and WANTING to do it are two very different things. I've just recently committed to growing my business from this place, which is requiring me to make some big changes:

- To let go of programs that have made me money but are no longer aligned with who I am — these things don't make sense logically, but it's time.
- To say no way more often than I say yes — it's been the other way around for years.
- To not use my "get it done" Generator energy as a way to avoid my calling — keeping myself doing and busy is a safe space for me, yet I can see where it's stunting my growth.
- To continue to acknowledge that deep success comes from who I am already — it's time to stop comparing myself to everyone else.

Paying attention to my gut so that I'm plugging my Generator energy into the right places has been (and continues to be!) one of the biggest lessons in my business and my life.

Figure 8. Tina Forsyth

Having worked online since 1999, Tina Forsyth is a 'jill of all trades' when it comes to running and growing a profitable service-based business. She is the author of the award-winning book, *The Entrepreneur's Trap*, and creator of the "CEO Business School for Transformational Leaders" where she teaches entrepreneurs her proven step-by-step process to set a strong foundation for business growth.

Tina also founded the International Association of Online Business Managers and is the creator of the Certified OBM™ Training, which is the only program of its kind to train high-end virtual managers. As an entrepreneur and recovering control-freak, Tina is passionate about sharing her experience and helping other entrepreneurs set up the right systems for teams and leveraged revenue streams that allow them to stop working so darn hard and have a business that can run without them (Woo Hoo!).

# Peg Rose Goddard

# Cave Woman

Cave Woman, according to Alison Armstrong from PAX, is the part of a woman's brain that keeps us hyper-vigilant. We don't want to kill her off because she helps us to survive. Cave Woman evolved when there were actual tigers in the woods that might eat us, and occasionally she takes over our brains and makes us do stupid things all in the name of survival. I know this, but it doesn't make the fear any less real. I know that the trick is to make a choice to rise up into Human Spirit.

So at 9:00 at night, I find myself crying hysterically in Arizona's Show Low Police Department with another 3 1/2 hour drive to Tucson, where a bed I have already paid for awaits me. A construction road sign says the road will be closed in another 1 1/2 hours near Globe, Arizona. I stopped here at the Police Department for help determining on which side of Globe the road was closed. Do I drive on or stop to spend the night?

But I need to start with the first part first. I became intrigued by Human Design when I discovered it was a combination of astrology, the Kabbala, Quantum Physics, and the I Ching. Back in the late 1970s, I worked as a commodity analyst for five years at HAL Commodity Trading Cycles using the theory of cycles (that history repeats itself). I researched the Seasonal Cycle for thirty-five different markets (and my research is now in college-level textbooks). We analyzed those thirty-five markets on a daily basis. Thirty-four of the thirty-five markets had approximately 28 to 29-Day Trading Cycles. My boss said. "Hmm... that looks like a lunar cycle. Someone in the office needs to learn astrology. Tag—you're it." That assignment led to my fascination with Astrology for the next 45 years. I believe that Astrology is the Ancients' way of cataloging cycles.

Astrology was able to explain most things in my life, but not everything. I had a fantastic personal astrologer for over a decade. I would get a yearly solar return update as a birthday present to myself. I had readings for my children within a month of their birth. This, along with the classes that I took, provided me with a wonderful foundation in Astrology. I considered these readings an incredible framework in which to function for the upcoming year, and the insights into my children were invaluable while they were growing up. (Unfortunately, my astrologist was in an auto accident, and for the next thirty years, I would miss her accurate insights into my life.)

Fast forward thirty years. I was in a marriage that was coming apart. My husband was depressed, controlling and drinking. However, he hadn't always been that way. I equated the situation to the story about boiling a frog. You put a frog in cold water and turn the temperature up one degree at a time. When I look back, the controlling started on our honeymoon. It was so gradual that I didn't really notice.

One day, I realized that I had given up all of my friends and I no longer talked with my family. Everyone was unacceptable for one reason or another. It had been easier to stop friendships than to deal with the consequences of keeping them. I was completely alone except for kids, work and husband. I decided I had to change this.

I got involved in a network marketing company and moved from one company to another as companies failed or didn't live up to their promises. I ended up eventually writing two different compensation plans. I was part of the advance team for the president of one company when we were opening up Asia. This was especially exciting for me since I had been born in the Philippines. The more successful I was outside of my marriage, the more depressed my husband became and the more he attempted to control me. After one night of a drunken rage (which he claimed to not remember), I began to be in fear of my life and for those of my two college-age kids who were still living at home.

The house began to resemble an armed siege camp: my youngest would no longer come downstairs when his father was awake. This meant he ate outside the home or brought food to eat in his room. Everyone retreated to their rooms and just "holed-up" and tiptoed around my husband. For almost a year I tried to figure out a way to get my husband to leave my family farm, but he wasn't leaving. I was told by others that I was under electronic surveillance and had been for quite some time. We discussed divorce and counseling. I knew that if we went to counseling that I would just be "wrong."

I suggested an alternative that might explain the dynamics within our relationship and help us to negotiate deals in order to keep the marriage intact. He agreed, so off I went to California for Alison Armstrong's PAX courses. We then took the four-day Couples Away class together. Things calmed down for six months. Deals that we had negotiated remained intact.

Then a 92-foot Blue Spruce pine tree fell on our house in the middle of the night on April 12, 2011. This triggered a series of events that would change everything. Within days, I was pushed down a set of stairs (not by my husband), forced to endure an eight-hour intervention organized by my husband, where I was specifically told upfront that "I could not defend myself" and berated for being a horrible selfish person. Six weeks later, my husband would express confusion, saying that he no longer knew whom to believe. Up until that point in time, he had never even asked to hear my side of the story!

I was done after the intervention. I recognized that I could do more for my kids by leaving than by staying. I called my dad the next day and told him that I needed a warehouse not in our town and not in my name. Then every day, after my husband went to work, I would pack up my car and take it to my warehouse. I started with the most valuable items and anything breakable that might get thrown in a rage. This went on for three months.

I still did not know where I was going to go or when, but I was getting prepared to leave. My dad was diagnosed with cancer. Then a friend asked me to house-sit. This gave me the perfect excuse. I told my husband that I was leaving, but this did NOT mean I was giving up my claim on our property. I was leaving because I no longer felt safe and I added, "Oh, by the way, stop your electronic surveillance." (Rumor has it that he was too addicted to this activity and it continued for a while.)

For months I changed locations every two weeks. I turned off the ability to locate me via phone or computer and changed all my passwords into Chinese. (Yes, Chinese... my best friend in high school had been born in Singapore.) It was almost two years before I could determine whether there was a keystroke program on my computer. My father offered to buy me a handgun with a laser sight and arrange for me to go through the conceal carry program for my own protection. I had friends who would keep my computer and cell phone at their house for days on end to throw off the surveillance. I even had one friend volunteer to drive my cellphone around the state for a week or two!

When it came time to file for divorce, the state I was living in was so weird that if the man didn't want a divorce, thanks to the "old boy network" it didn't happen. I know women who had waited ten, fifteen or twenty years to get a divorce. Usually, this only happens when their soon-to-be ex has found someone else they wanted to marry. Therefore, it became important to find a state where I could be domiciled for divorce purposes but not lose my residency in the other state due to the family farm.

By this time, my astrologer had returned to doing readings. I asked for an astrology reading specifically about the divorce, and she was consulting not only our two charts but those of our two sons. She told me that it would take over three years. And I cried. She warned me about a six-month period in which to not to even contact my husband "unless I wanted to look over my shoulder for the rest of my life in every dark parking lot." She warned me to go slow and "not poke the cobra" if I wanted to accomplish my goal of my kids and I being alive at the end of the process.

In December 2014, I heard about Human Design and found a facilitator with whom I could have a reading. She had my husband's and my charts and told me things that Astrology had never revealed. She explained that because he was a Manifestor, I needed to just inform him. She explained how asking questions could make him feel defensive and lead to his pattern of just being "locked up" emotionally. She confirmed things using our Human Design charts that I had suspected about our relationship.

I started taking Human Design classes, and to me, Human Design is like Astrology on steroids. There is so much depth in this system. No matter what class I took, I learned things that explained relationships, patterns, and my life. I couldn't get enough information.

I was finally settled enough to focus on my divorce and take another class. Human Design was still calling to me, so I decided to a take a class called Abundance by Design and become a facilitator. Out of the blue, I got a call from a friend asking me if I wanted to sell the family farm. Apparently, a family member was suddenly moving back to the county five years earlier than expected and wanted to farm. Her mom took her around to see everything that was on the market and, on a whim, showed her mine. The daughter fell in love with my farm and hence the question.

Her first question on November 30th was where I was in my divorce, and I told her that it was supposed to be finalized the next day. She laughed and said that was good because she did not want to upset that process.

I had never even thought about selling the farm since it came down from my dad's side of the family. It had been in my family since the time of the American Revolution, and it was assumed that I would pass it on to my children. However, in the years since I had not been living there because I felt unsafe, my husband had allowed the home to deteriorate. There was no functioning heater, and many of the windows were cracked or missing. Multiple cats were accustomed to peeing and pooping wherever they wished in the back part of the house that was occupied by my husband since he stopped cleaning out the litter box several years previously.

Now you have to understand that the state where this farm was located has been very depressed. The downturn in our economy happened around 2000.

Only two farms had sold in the county in the previous seven years. The house was falling down (practically unlivable) and I get a full cash offer for what the farm was appraised for two years earlier!

Miracle? Yes! Did my Abundance by Design class have anything to do with these events? Absolutely!

So now I was selling the family farm. I used Abundance by Design and Healing by Human Design every step of the way. It took me only six weeks to deal with surveyors and attorneys and move my husband into a house that he purchased. I even had the guts to inform him that I was tired of seeing his handgun next to his keyboard every time I had to walk through his office into the kitchen. I said that I didn't care if he put it into a desk drawer, I would still know that the handgun was there. I just could no longer function at the level I needed seeing it lying there all the time. I informed, and he performed. Miracle!

And yes, I got the divorce the next day. It was almost a five-year process. I had to drive over 1,200 miles to get every piece of paper signed. I did not return to my family farm unless one of my sons was there for protection, and I never gave my husband any warning. I would only meet him in public places like restaurants or banks.

I have used Human Design to help navigate so many different relationships. My current fiance has an elderly mother who does not always remember things clearly. His desire is for her to continue to utilize her brain, so he asks open-ended questions in the Socratic Method, which he loves. Since she is a Generator, she needs to be asked yes-and-no questions. The more questions he asks, the more confused she gets, and she tends to just shut down rather than make any decisions. This has led to numerous uncomfortable evenings. He marvels at how I can get things back on track by simply asking questions that require just a yes or no.

She is also at a point where some old, painful memories resurface. In the past, we have endured days and weeks of her rehashing the old story in painful details, which led to weeks of depression and no desire to even get out of bed. Using Healing by Human Design and Emotional Freedom Technique (EFT) tapping, I have tapped on everything from specific incidents to bad dreams that she can't even remember. I end the sessions with affirming her positive outlook and positive memories. A recent session around anger with her sister ended with her suddenly remembering a funny story from when they were very young. Even my fiance has started using the EFT tapping with her when I am not around.

Other good things continued to come into my life with Human Design, too. In the Fall of 2015, I had no idea where I was going next with regards to my career. My father had died, and I had spent nine months helping people move out of their homes. When people asked what I did for a living, I merely said that I was in transition. As a Projector, I knew that I had to be recognized for my talents and invited into the next phase of my life. In the meantime, it was important to continue to learn and put myself out there to the public.

And back to my evening in Arizona, the one that is the same night as the day I attempted to get a driver's license in my new name now that my divorce is finalized. Ahead of me, I have a five-day Healing by Human Design Level 3 Certification that starts first thing in the morning. I am heading into the middle of nowhere (few towns or gas stations) on a winding road I've never seen, in the dark, with the potential of deer or other wild animals on the road.

I am not prepared like I usually am for getting caught in the middle of nowhere in my car: no jugs of water, no extra blanket, not even a long-sleeve, heavy shirt, much less my ankle-length down parka to keep me warm in the 45-degree weather should I break down (or, again, hit an animal in the dark).

I am in the middle of a "Cave Woman" attack. I have been driving for 5 1/2 hours and crying for most of it, including two hours when I could not stop. I have already survived a snow storm with icicles on the trees and massive rain. My brain knows logically that I am fine; the deer are not tigers that will eat me, but Cave Woman has taken over and convinced my brain and my body that I will not survive this. I am doomed.

Today, the trigger for this "attack" is that I am finally divorced after a difficult five-year process. Just that morning, I was attempting to change my name. In order to do so, I had to prove where I was living. I have been in hiding for so long I don't have the necessary documents to prove that I live anywhere. Bank accounts are in a physical address from three locations ago. My driver's license is in a property that has been sold and I have no connection to anymore.

Sometimes, we just plain forget the tools that we have in our toolboxes. We are so buried in our emotional junk that we just plain get stupid. This is when we need friends and coaches to remind us of our magnificence. I find that these brain blocks usually happen just about the time when we have reached a very deep core issue and are ready to release it. It's what I had been using with my to-be mother-in-law and I needed to refocus it for me.

I also studied a magnificent technique called Healing by Human Design. It is a marvelous mixture of Human Design and the EFT tapping, using your Human Design chart as a guide to what emotional issues to tap. It focuses on some really deep core issues, including the Nine Resiliency Keys: nine traits that must be in place in order to bounce back. I had come up against two of these: Lovability and Self Worth. In my personal session out tumbled issues that I had thought I had previously resolved, about people and incidents that I was under the illusion I had completely forgiven.

There wasn't a memory of these things. I have discovered that Core issues often need to be cleared three times: on the Conscious, Subconscious and Body levels. I had consciously forgiven these people and incidents. My personal session had rooted out the fact that my unconscious had not been completely engaged during the forgiveness process. This particular "Cave Woman" attack was the final layer... my body and limbic brain's visceral response on a survival level.

We often need something quick and easy to turn the tide of emotions. So, after leaving the police department, I started EFT tapping about anything I can think of to calm down the rage of my Cave Woman, reminding myself that I deeply and completely love and accept myself.

Once the emotions have subsided, I go to the local Target store and purchase two jugs of water, two long-sleeved, heavy shirts, tennis shoes, and a sleeping bag. Cave Woman is now satisfied that if the worst should happen, I will not die of thirst or freeze to death and, if necessary, I can hike out to a remote house or the nearest town on the Navajo Reservation. I drive off into the night not sure whether the road past Globe will be open or not.

That night in Tucson, I was able to completely clear the rest of the Cave Woman attack events as well as all the incidents that surfaced during my session with the facilitator. I went from being afraid and being in hiding to being willing to write about all of this for publication. Talk about coming out of hiding in a Big Way!

Trust your Healing by Human Design practitioner. Be willing to be vulnerable and tell the ugly things that you are inclined to hide. We all have shameful things in our past. You will probably get to the root eventually anyway with Human Design. However, there is no sense in the process taking longer than necessary. Healing by Human Design and Abundance by Design take time, but they are faster and much deeper than anything else I have experienced. I am healed of traumas that have held me captive emotionally and financially for over forty years. The Freedom is Miraculous!

Figure 9. Peg Rose Goddard

Peg Rose has lived in three different houses with weird energy in the last 35+ years, including one with an ancient curse in addition to another connected to murder and malevolent spirits. Out of necessity, she learned how (and now specializes in) cleansing homes and properties. Peg Rose's journey to heal herself and others led her to learn various techniques including Inter-Dimensional Work and PAX's Noble Healing and Noble Forgiveness.

She is a licensed Human Design Facilitator for Abundance by Design and Healing by Human Design, Level Three. Her areas of emphasis are healing traumas from sexual, physical and emotional abuse, being a midwife to the creativity of the Divine Feminine and creating Divine Partnership through collaboration with the Divine Masculine.

Peg Rose managed family farms for more than 35 years, donating a portion of the land and property for a Montessori school in 1997, where she spent twelve years as a teacher and assistant; she then sold the rest of the land in 2016. She has served as Treasurer for a 50i(c)3 non-profit organization for 30 years started by her best friend to work with Native American youth and elders.

After being in hiding for five years, Peg Rose is happily living and investing in Real Estate in the Rocky Mountains in Divine Partnership with her partner, who was secretly in love with her for 43 years.

# Rebekkah Hanson

## Unmask

Abundance comes in many forms. It can indicate copious amounts of friends, experiences, good fortune, talents, food and even includes money. The common denominator is each and every one of us has a reference in how we experience each form of abundance.

We are all born with a unique genetic blueprint that contains the basic characteristics of who we are physically, mentally, emotionally and spiritually. Most of our parents didn't have a handbook on how to raise their children; teachers and school systems have been in the same predicament. Society as a whole doesn't have the guidance how to use the individualized gifts we bring to the planet. As such, we learned in our early childhood how to mask ourselves to gain acceptance. As a result, a disconnect happens. This disconnect then becomes a misaligned version of who we are as well as the potential we hold and leaves us in a struggle. We are out of alignment. That misalignment often manifests as a lack of abundance.

Getting people back into that alignment has been my goal. Whether it's personal, parental or relationship, the first thing is that alignment. It's the most important first step. For business owners, that piece is key. The alignment and reconnection to their original birth code is huge because once they have learned their strengths with their Strategy to play out that strength, there is a choice to align with their greatness. There is no more hiding. Awareness makes it so much easier to step into an abundant way of existing.

This is the piece where Human Design really helped me. We were all born perfect, different and as a unique piece of the puzzle that unites the consciousness of our planet as a whole. Human Design system simplifies everything and gives your Strategy and Authority. You can be that unique piece of the whole that you were meant to be. You can study for years before understanding all the intricate layers of Human Design, but even a novice can glean useable nuggets that help you become the person you were created to be.

In my practice I use Human Design as one of three modalities; the other two I use are Astrology and Numerology. I've been an Astrologer for over forty years and started incorporating Human Design and Numerology in the past few years. The three facets work beautifully together — my clients have responded and grown as a result. Each human has such a beautiful potential.

Once a client reaches the awareness of that potential, I've found they are frequently in tears because they have been touched deeply. It brings them back to who they essentially are, how they were born into this world, and reminds them that it's okay to be authentic. It brings that soul destiny path into their hands and they realize that's what they are here to do whereas, in the past, destiny escaped them as it seems too easy.

My story started in the early 1970's while I was living in northeastern Kentucky. My brother-in-law approached me and said he was going to introduce me to someone. As this man shook my hand, he said, "I'm here to teach you Astrology."

He proceeded to come over every couple of weeks and give me assignments. For me, it was like remembering and was very easy to learn. I picked up all the little nuances right away. But being in that part of the country, I took quite a bit of criticism (downright verbal abuse), which drove me into a closet with my modality. I hid my knowledge while I kept studying.

During my second marriage (still in Kentucky), I found myself in a very difficult situation. As a result of a couple of fairly severe accidents, my husband spent about five years cycling in and out of deep depression that included multiple suicide attempts (though when we parted ways, he still had not succeeded). It wasn't long before I started comparing the celestial cycles to the ups and downs of his emotional well-being. I found these times remarkably parallel to the planetary transits as they cycled in relation to his natal birth chart.

This was an extremely dramatic time in my life and took its toll on me for sure, but the gift in hindsight was that I recognized my gift. I was able to really study the cyclical effects and how he chose to respond or react to them. Though I'm a firm believer that consciousness is above all else, when you are aware of the timing of things, you can use these modalities to gain insight. You can see what kind of climate will be in effect or what the celestial weather may be like; it gives you the opportunity to respond, react, and design your own response.

The real learning from that period in my life was being able to see the cyclical patterns we experience. I now use my knowledge helping people align the timing of events after their personal growth piece is in place because that's where the abundance lives.

My studies of Astrology continued as I moved to Colorado, although I kept my modality a secret for a good ten years after the move. Finally at a party one night, I had brought my computer and asked the host if I could do a few "off the cuff" readings. I sat for six hours with person after person at the corner of the room. I was so focused on what I was doing that I didn't notice they set a fishbowl on my table for tips; my secret life was finally known. The abundance that followed prompted me to call myself a professional. That fishbowl was a great analogy as I was finally seen.

I've been doing Astrology now for more than forty years. About the same time as I began including Numerology, people started asking if I used Human Design. This question became so common I felt like I was being pursued to investigate it. What I found was that it rounded out my practice with clients and I was able to give them tools to help express their already perfect design. It really pulled it all together and was amazing. I felt Human Design pursued me just as Astrology had done decades earlier. It kept whispering in my ear, tapping me on my shoulder as if to say, "You need to do this!" Abundance comes in many forms.

One step lead to another and before I knew it, I was learning Human Design. Now I use it for all my clients. Because Astrology is a very integral part of it (and I already understood the various cycles of planetary energies), I fell in love with it. Astrology is ancient and used by U.S. Presidents, Wall Street financiers and is one subtly kept secret. But I think the cat is out of the bag and Human Design is also swiftly gaining credibility. Being part of accelerating that knowledge is such an honor.

For me, a 2/4 Generator, I know I must respond. Sometimes it takes me a while, but awareness has set in and the conscious act of waiting to respond has made my life so much easier (as well as abundant). Giving my clients the tools for their best strategy has achieved that for them, too. Helping them step into the higher version of themselves is a real honor and so very humbling.

Before, in my own journey I always felt I was too strong. After realizing how to step into that power, I was able to remove the cloak that hid me once when I felt the freedom to be myself. At that point, I started getting comments from others indicating they felt more at ease around me. I was guided on how to step fully into my power so I could fulfill what I came to do as a person on this planet. And I can use this to help others.

I have a client (6/2 Generator), crippled by fear most of her life. At first, she struggled to show her real face to the world. She was a loner with a gift that she was afraid to share. After recognizing how she was designed and bravely practicing her gifts in private, she now shares that publicly and her wisdom is seen.

Another client (4/6 Manifestor with a defined Will Center) was not allowing herself to rest regularly. Exhaustion was preventing her from her life-long work. She felt angry, not being able to force her way to completion of her project. Once she realized how to align with her Design, the flow and ease appeared. When I brought in the astrological cycles, it helped her to see rest/work timing for her was important.

When you help a client get that foundation of inner-aligning to your authenticity, it helps give them a principle for successful and abundant living. It's inspiring. Each person has their wisdom to share. It's magical to watch the growth that happens once they really step into that place of core knowing. It's going to be an amazing world when we get to the tipping point of most everyone using these tools. The people that are already empowered to live according to their Strategy are starting to throw their nugget of knowledge into the pond making a ripple. It is going to be amazing once we all have gained that insight.

I would love to see Human Design used in schools, giving students a solid start. From time to time, I work with parents. I have been told more than once that using Human Design has made a difference in being able to communicate with their child or teenager. I empower every parent I can.

Once I find that my clients are really ready to develop their true core strength, I usually give them some homework. As they are inspired to really delve into their true core strength, it just takes a little nudge to help them soar. Usually, my clients are searching because:

- They are unhappy.
- They are going through relationship changes.
- They find themselves wanting to grow and their relationship seems to be going a different direction.
- They have some kind of conflict between what they have and what they want.
- They are not satisfied at work.
- They feel like they always have to push for what they get.

There's a process of validating that is very helpful when they've been wearing that mask of "imprinting" and living someone else's expectations. Once they see and choose to be themselves, there is a freedom that takes place. It's as if they can finally see what makes them fully alive and express their own truth.

It's as if they realize, "Yeah, that's right. That's who I really am." Things start to change. What doesn't align seems to drop off (from a job that doesn't fit them, a relationship that is mis-aligned or family members' expectations). I've seen it so many times in so many different areas including people trying to live a gender that's not authentic.

In my practice, I always say that when we look at core design, it's going to prompt questions. I'm really supporting the transformational process. I want people to be able to integrate this into their lives.

In another example of working with a client, during one of her follow-up sessions, she informed me she felt blocked and couldn't "bust through." She had a goal in mind, but fears were paralyzing as well as sabotaging her progress. After explaining the lower expression of some of the Gates in her Spleen Center that exemplified those fears, it let her know that the higher expressing could move past those. That gave her the information she needed, and she did beautifully.

That awareness alone helped her step into her ease of flow. This person was a Generator with an emotional Authority and had an Incarnation Cross of Limitations. She was working hard trying to keep a positive mindset, but she was working with the lower energy of Gate 44 (fear of repeating old mistakes) when she really had a 'nose for truth.' Her gifts should serve her well when she was making a sale. Abundance can be hers. She had been held back as a child and can now let that go.

Assigning tools to use when the old dragons would emerge is always helpful. Journaling, documenting emotional fluctuations and using a few affirmations to help lift people out of the valley can help change trajectory.

I use visual screen sharing technology to help my clients see on their Astrology and Human Design charts what is happening, sharing that cycles always come and go. Being flexible with these cycles brings freedom and abundance. Living by your Strategy, Authority and learning how to use the definition in addition to openness in your body graph aligns you with your power. It fits you with the knowledge to be able to make decisions correctly and your life easier. The result is abundance in all areas.

Figure 10. Rebekkah Hanson

Rebekkah Hanson has been an Astrologer for more than forty years and is certified in Human Design and Numerology. The passion Rebekkah brings to her client's results in transformation. She reconnects them with the truth of who they are and their mission in life, helping them to understand how they can navigate life challenges to get past the struggles as well as guiding them to understand what is truly valuable, meaningful, and worth "the fight." As this alignment occurs, abundance follows.

An insight from one of Rebekkah's clients shares the connection she is able to foster:

*"I left our call having this interesting and clear sense of what my true North really is. I had a knowing of it on some level before our call, but something about hearing Rebekkah tell me things about myself made the hairs on the back of my neck stand up in the oddest of ways. It was like all the things I knew from life were validated in an hour long call. I felt this confidence to pursue my business with the awareness that this is what I am on this planet to do. I frequently look over the notes from our call just in case I missed something."* KW

Rebekkah is a speaker, teacher, author and mentor with an international clientele. She lives in the Denver, Colorado area.

# Linda Bissin Copp

# Know Yourself

I had been a managing family therapist for almost 30 years. I was pretty frustrated because I'd been working with people for so long and couldn't figure out why some of the things that work for some people didn't work for others. I really love my clients and wanted to help them. Having them stay challenged for as long as they were -I knew they were stuck. Something had to work.

A very dear friend of mine I've known now for almost 40 years came to me, and Judith said, "I think you should have a Human Design reading. I think you'd really find this fascinating." I said I would and did. It turns out that I was not happy because I learned I am a Projector with a 2/4 Profile. I was absolutely positive after what I had read that I was probably a Manifesting Generator. I work like crazy all the time; there was no stopping me or slowing me down. I just thought the Human Design specialist was wrong and that can't be me. That's not how I've lived my whole life.

Projectors couldn't do what I do in terms of the way that I work, but I've always worked for myself. I pace myself. I've tried working for other people when I was very young in my 20's and it just didn't work. I went back to school, got my degree and started working with clients. I also volunteered at the local hospital with what they called "The Pink Ladies" and gave one thousand hours in one year. I was always moving, always working and I had children. I'm doing all the things that people do when they run a home: grocery shopping, housecleaning, cooking, washing, ironing and all those things along with going to school, working at the clinic and doing volunteer work. So tell me that's not a Manifesting Generator!

From the time I was born, there was nothing suggesting what might make a difference in my chart because of the way that I was living. Now, mind you, I came from a family where I have three brothers, a mother and a father. Mother was a Generator, Dad was a Manifesting Generator and all my brothers were Generators. When you're in a situation like that, you're just basically conditioned to *be* that. This is who you are. You do this.

Because mom had to work and so did dad in order for us to manage, I assumed the responsibility of some of the household duties as the oldest child and the only girl. Never did I have any of the fatigue, burn out and all the things that they talk about for Projectors. The women I know who are Projectors just could not function if they had to do that much. Others like me could do just about anything they wanted. I didn't know what the difference was except now I know I was conditioned to believe that is how you live.

In talking with the Human Design specialist, I explained to her that this just didn't fit, didn't feel right. Being the very kind and understanding person that she is said, "Well, this is your correct information, that's right about you and you might want to explore that." I wasn't going to have any part of that, so we talked further and I told her that when I was 28 years old I had a near death experience after the birth and death of my third child.

I asked her if it was a possibility that the near-death experience might be the reason things change for me. I gave her the time and the date and the place that that happened and sure enough, it came up as a Manifesting Generator. I don't even remember the Profile. I felt at peace. I was curious, thinking that perhaps this could help my clients.

I started studying Human Design and the deeper I got into those first classes, the more it became very clear that I was indeed a Projector. In a way, it was a great relief because I have a 2/4 Profile and I have a tendency to be quite a hermit. I used to feel very badly about that because I wasn't real social. I didn't like to be out among people. I'm not shy. It's just that it was uncomfortable for me. Understanding that's a trait a 2/4 Profile would have, I felt so relieved.

Along with that, my chart is mostly open; I only have three Centers defined: in the head, the Ajna and the Throat (very few channels activated at all). I'm grateful for that because it helped me understand over the years why I was able to tune into my clients so quickly. I could understand even before they did what challenges they were having so that I could direct our conversations in ways that they would get to the problems quicker and be done with counseling.

From the point of the reading, I was able to say to my clients if we can't resolve the issues that you're here for within a certain period of time then I'm not the therapist for you. The longest I would stay with a client would be about 18 months. I started doing charts for all my clients and it was amazing how changes happened more quickly. I was able to work with them as their Type and their Profile using their Strategy as opposed to trying to figure those traits out (which would take a while).

It made my work more efficient because if you can look at a person's chart you know where to start. You don't have to try and figure that part out. Here's their Type, here's their Strategy and their Profile. That's a lot of information right there. They begin to understand how they operate and what their Strategy is because I shared that information with them and it helped them to really get a grip on their life. I think the Strategy is key for everyone, because if you just try it out, you'll see changes. They'll come back every time and say, "I can't believe the difference, how much easier things are for me."

I could see the difference, particularly with Projectors with their need to communicate what they're feeling and what they know. If no one has recognized their wisdom or has not asked for what they know, they're not going to be heard. In my particular work, people would always ask me questions and they wanted my opinions. Being invited was natural in what I was doing. Giving information to them was a natural thing to do. It wasn't me waiting to be invited or asked; they ask me.

Sharing information with them about what they could do to help themselves made a big difference and allowed them to finish their time with me a lot quicker. For people who are the fast movers (like the Manifesting Generators and Generators), basically they take the information and some of them will really grab onto it. Others will just kind of say "uh-huh" and then they'll come back later with some stories that literally change how they operate completely. Everybody has a story that will help show them that they can change if they just do *this*.

There are others, though, that have Sacral Inner Authority and can't hear the Sacral energy in their design. Through Human Design, I learned how to make a list of questions I can ask them so that they can learn how to hear the response of their Sacral. That was a wonderful lesson because it works. It all works if you just do it.

Human Design was basically a gift to me because a couple of years before I found it via my friend, Judith, I had gone through a particularly hard time in my life. Human Design gave me a deep understanding of the things that change in your life and that it is not the end. You're just moving forward into the next part of life. And so I approached everything using Human Design — even in my relationship, including my new relationships.

When I started using Human Design, I started paying more attention to me and not what was outside of me. I started paying attention to how I actually felt, the sleep patterns that I had and the way that I would go to sleep at night. I was doing a lot of things that Projectors do just naturally and one of them was the way that I would sleep. If I went to bed exhausted, I wouldn't sleep, just toss and turn all night. But if I would go to bed before I was exhausted, relax, read, then turn the light off, I would go to sleep right away.

I also noticed my 2/4 Profile, always having an excuse not to be out there except with my children and when I could do something for someone else. The transition to accepting my projector self wasn't immediate. It was just something that I started watching and let myself be. Before Human Design, I wouldn't let myself be that person who rested in between events during the day, someone who took the time to just be kind to myself and to look at what I was doing: I was managing. I was managing my life, which is what Projectors do. It was just me looking at the different aspects of my chart that make up my Type and my unique Human Design.

Although I worked like a Manifesting Generator my whole life, I knew I was more patient than most Generators or Manifesting Generators, and that's not typical. I don't think I've ever talked to one of those Types that didn't interrupt me when I was talking and say, "Well, let's get to the bottom-line here." I would tell them that the Generator Types aren't known for their patience and that comment usually makes them laugh. So that's kind of the way it was for me. It wasn't an 'aha' moment. It was me looking at me and finally surrendering, then being relieved that I didn't have to be that Type (because a Manifesting Generator is like a whirling dervish).

Once I started Human Design, I studied everything I could find. I bought all the books, read them until the pages are just about worn out. If you don't understand the concept it isn't because you're not intelligent. It's because it hasn't resonated yet. It hasn't really moved down into your heart or it hasn't integrated enough. One day, you'll wake up in the morning and have a clear understanding. But, sometimes it doesn't work like that. Sometimes you're in the middle of doing something and you think it's your big idea when it's really something your Human Design specialist had explained months' ago. When you're actively involved with Human Design for a long time and consider retirement, you think, *"How can I stop?"* You never know when a person is going to come along and ask you if you really think Human Design will help them; I tell them that it changed my life completely, and I have confidence it will help them to change theirs.

I've always felt we need more Human Design Specialists. We need more people who will share this because each of us will find who we are designed to be. The beauty of who we really are and I feel like the more of us there are the better for humanity.

I have one particular client, "Joyce." She called me almost two years ago and her words were, "I'm desperate. I need some help." I did her chart for her and she came back a week later and saying she needed to know more. I've been working with her Human Design now for almost two years and she said that it's the only thing that keeps her going. She has a lot of challenges, such as:

- She's an MS patient.
- She had lost her sight.
- She had lost her bladder control.
- She still has difficulty walking; one leg is completely paralyzed.
- She can't sit up for any length of time - she has to be flat.
- She was raised with religious dogma that taught her from the time she was born to turn the other cheek.

Because Joyce is a very genuine, loving person, and lived her life to always look out for the other person, be like Christ, and she took it to heart. It was not what's wrong with them, but always what am I doing wrong to cause that behavior?

Human Design changed all that for her. It gave her insight into her husband (whose design is a Manifestor) and why he was not informing her when he did things that might cause her great distress. She learned to look at his chart and really understand that based on how he was raised, his conditioning by his family, the world in general, the way that his chart is configured and him living in his "not-self" that his behavior wasn't personal. She once believed, *"There's something wrong with me that can't be right."* She thought everything that happened in her life that did not serve her meant there was something wrong with her. Now understanding her design she knows that is not true.

Learning about herself, she now knows that she is a 6/2 Profile and is a Projector. She understands that she is an amazing human being with tremendous insights. She has completely healed herself of many things and she's quite a researcher. Having done so much research, she changed her diet, regained her sight, and regained her bladder control. Human Design also really helped Joyce understand her family — her mother, who completely rejected her for her whole life, and her sister, who isolated herself. Both are no longer with us, but Joyce has calmed her soul. Looking at her Chart, she was able to undo the way she looked at things and has completely let go of religious dogma. Joyce has moved into her true spiritual self and let go of the torture of guilt-producing experience.

She has only the first three Centers defined and the rest of Centers in her chart are open. She's extremely intuitive and has learned to trust that via Human Design. She is so open that she basically a true empath and feels all of the chaos that's going on now. That's part of her challenge that she's trying to change, to learn to understand what's hers and what's not and what to do with those things.

In Joyce's words:

*On a bleak November 2013 evening, little did I know that I was a 6/2 Projector who had had a great fall and had not been put back together Again. I was dealing with a progressive and virulent auto-immune Disease - Multiple Sclerosis along with Celiac Disease and other Physical miseries. In addition, I had experienced the deaths of a number of close family members and in the chaos the drifting away, and loss Of all my friends.*

*I was feeling deep despair and the sense that my life was useless and I longed for it to be over. The physical, mental, and spiritual pain was All encompassing and I had little hope or sense of where to find relief.*

*I was 63 and wondered why my life was in such a desolate state when all I had really lived or wanted to do was to make some difference in the World and to truly alleviate some small bit of suffering. (My 50th, 29th, And 8th Gates were all alive but not well, having been active and conditioned In the worst ways).*

*As I perused online Astrology books that stormy night I was looking for some small nugget of hope to keep me going. That nugget of hope Appeared for me in the guise of Understanding Human Design by Karen Curry. It was not your "typical" Astrology book but something about it caught my attention. Thus began and continues to be one of the most Exciting, invigorating and healing journeys of my life. (I can never thank You enough Karen.). After reading Karen's book and seeing an HD chart, I was seared to the depths of my soul. I knew I had to have a reading and a coach but who, and how? Finances were tight and I felt so vulnerable to interact with a stranger in such a deep way.*

*In early December I found Linda Bissin-Copp's website Human Design 4 Life and took the plunge. Unbeknownst to me, I had hit the Motherlode, My reading was incredible. It is truly amazing to have someone hundreds of miles away know who you truly are and believe in the real you. Someone you have never met! Something I had never experienced before in my whole life. I cried and cried knowing that the little quiet whispers throughout the years of who I Truly was were not a mirage. My reading was also backed up by a very comprehensive, well-written report. I read it over and over Again, and still do when I need a reminder of who I am.*

*So the journey had begun and continued with coaching every week. It was the highlight of my week and continues to be to this very day. Linda Introduced me to Karen Curry's wonderful courses and guided me to the most exciting, breathtaking and liberating knowledge. She has quite a resume besides her HD expertise. She has studied many Spiritual Disciplines and also has an MA in Counseling. What a Divine combo and God knows I needed it! (so many people who are fortunate enough to discover HD are quite bereft, lost and bleeding). Linda patiently, lovingly and wisely guided me along the way and has never given up on me. She deeply loves HD and is a True counselor, one of those rare and special Souls that do their work out of love and really know what they are doing. And, she is the most nonjudgmental person I have ever known. She helped me to believe and delight in myself again. Not an easy task.*

*I have learned so many things these last few years and with the Gate 481 will continue my quest as I want to get to the depths of the Well and it will not be work. It is the most exciting trek I have ever experienced.*

*Linda taught me, with the backup of HD that nothing is personal. When one realizes that to their core, the knowing is priceless. What liberation!*

*I'm also learning how to navigate in this unique costume surrounding me, and rebelling less and Less. When one understands their Strategy and Profile and why they are the way they are, life becomes so much easier and the internal criticism begins to lessen. (A lengthy process) And, speaking of Compassion, HD, helps one see the unique and special qualities of each person's design. If everyone had access to this information the World would be a very different place. When each person is really seen and valued for who they truly are and lovingly assisted in their unique growth and talents much of the despair and anger of the World dissipates. Also, each person's quirks become understandable, sometimes, even lovable. Who would've thought?!!! The quirks may even bind us together. Yes, it is true, well, sometimes. :)*

*With these words, I am just skimming the periphery of the gifts of HD. The gifts of Linda are vast also and she has walked with me, week by week every step of the way, Through some very difficult times and some joyous ones as well. Much of the joy has come from our learning together and I have no words adequate to express my gratitude to her.*

*As for me, there are still times of despair and frustration but mainly due To the paralysis and anomalies of MS. My Spirit, my identity, my Soul, My self-esteem grow stronger and stronger. Maybe in time my body will follow suit. I long for that day. I may be a "late bloomer" but all the twists and turns on this journey have gifted me with immense treasures I wish to share.*

*With much gratitude and many Blessings,*
*Thank you Linda, Thank you Karen and Thank you HD .*
*Joyce S.*

I've also worked with a woman named "Cari." She is a Projector with a 1/3 Profile, and she's really more of a social person, very intelligent, a member of Mensa and a successful artist. She's very conscious, with a lot of awareness, and has spent her life trying to improve herself. She has schooled herself in many different spiritual things that have been transformative for her and that have helped her evolve her consciousness.

For instance, she was in a relationship with a gentleman who was abusive and felt stuck because she didn't have a way to help herself move out of the relationship. Yet she's a beautiful artist. Prior to settling into painting full time, she traveled the world doing interior design, traveling all over Europe and the United States. When she called me, she was like many of my clients: desperate. I shared her Human Design with her; everything that she had told me about herself was right there in the chart.

She has the Throat, Identity, Will (heart) and Spleen Center. She is curious about everything and always wants to know everything. When I shared with her some of the possibilities in her chart that would allow her to move forward, she took them to heart. It took her a while. Once she got back on her feet and started doing her artwork again, she told her significant other he had to leave.

I've been talking to her for three years now and a year ago, she reconnected with a man that she has known and been friends with for 20 years. Their timing was always off so they were never together, but they had always been attracted to one another. They rekindled their relationship, fell deeply in love and married. She has a happy ending.

That's just the short version of her story. Moving out of that unhappy relationship took some time, yet she moved forward and changed her life with the help of her Human Design.

In Cari's words:

*At a particularly challenging time of my life, a friend of mine told me about the Human Design consultation that he once had with Linda Bissin-Copp. He said that he found it quite helpful in his endeavor to understand himself better. I had always been intrigued by the I Ching, Astrology, Quantum Physics and mildly curious about the Kabbalah, so I decided to explore.*

*Like most people who have a reading with Linda, they are suddenly faced with the wonderful task of processing a lot of new information about themselves. Ever since my young adulthood, I had been pondering the great questions of who am I, where did I come from, why am I here and where am I going? Understanding my Human Design was certainly one of the greatest quantum leaps in my realization of who I am.*

*I was absolutely fascinated by Linda's ability to know more about me than I did in some ways, just by knowing when and where I was born. I had always been fascinated with the concept of self-realization, and this cosmology appeared to be nothing short of magic! I gave a humble thank you to this wonderful woman who was to later become my best friend. Then I went off to contemplate the amazing 30 page written report of information that she had given me after an hour and a half phone consultation.*

*Although I occasionally had a psychic or astrological reading at times in my life, this was a whole other adventure into understanding myself. I couldn't stop thinking about it, so I called Linda and asked her how she learned how to do this and could we explore more. Although I was absolutely fascinated by the intricacy and accuracy of the report Linda had given me, I was equally as fascinated by Linda's personality and intuitiveness.*

*Something told me that she was the loftiest person I had ever met; I wanted to know more about who she was and Human Design. I asked her if she would be willing to teach me. After I had met and talked with some other teachers, I realized that Linda was definitely the one that I resonated with the most. I was absolutely delighted to be embarking on a journey that would and has changed my life in many wonderful ways.*

*Linda was so encouraging, that I always felt great about the information that I was learning and the patient pace at which she so lovingly shared these pearls of wisdom. The first realization was a confirmation of much of who I already suspected and accepted myself to be. The second was the challenge of seeing and accepting the parts of me that I was somewhat unaware of, and not particularly pleased about.*

*As time went by, I realized that Linda had indeed been the outrageous person that I suspected, and together we watched this new knowledge begin to transform my world.*

*My relationships also began to be totally transformed. I reached a whole new level of empathy for my friends. My love relationships reflected that as well. My love and compassion for my daughters grew exponentially as I gained a deeper understanding of Human Design.*

*I also gained insights regarding my significant other that inspired me to totally rethink how I see love. In fact, it completely changed my love relationship. I finally understood, in no uncertain terms, why I could never find peace or happiness with the person that I had been involved with for many years. Fortunately, as I made my decisions regarding this relationship, the love of my life / soul mate, finally surfaced and moved our 20-year-old friendship into the happiest marriage I could have ever imagined.*

*Human Design has given me an exquisitely perfect explanation of who I am, and how to navigate my life optimally. I can honestly say, I feel very blessed to have had the good fortune to meet Linda, and to learn about, how to greatly improve my life by living my unique Human Design.*

*Cari T.*

I think when you with work with Human Design as long as I have (almost 10 years) that it's like peeling an onion— it just goes deeper and deeper and deeper. It's something that is absolutely amazing to me.

Here's another example of what a reading can do for someone:

One day a young man called me and he hadn't been outside for almost a year. He was just about ready to call "this thing called life" off. I did his chart for him and talked to him about his Type and Strategy and about the other things in his chart and encouraged him to start to go out of his apartment starting with just a short walk and going a little further each day he agreed to do that, took his newly acquired information to think about and we said our goodbyes. Two weeks later I got a letter from him that said that this "Human Design" thing changed his whole life. He had been going out of his apartment and he's looking into other things instead of doing the same things in his life. He was a stock trader, now he felt life was worth living and that he could find a way to be happy.

Personally, I have used Human Design in my own family, too. Four of my children are Generator Types, one is a Projector and my youngest is a Manifestor. So just right there, I had my own test field and learning about how to talk with them, speak with them, and offer things to them. Working with my Manifestor child was magical because I never said no to her. What I would do when she a young child would be to divert her attention with play and other interesting things. As she got older, I never gave her a reason to not tell me what she was doing. Now she informs me (and the world) what's going on with her because of my little experiment.

With my Projector daughter, she was clearly conditioned to be a Manifesting Generator like her mama thought she was. Teaching her and working with her over the last nine years has really helped her get rid of a lot of her anxiety, to allowed her to breathe, to sleep when she needs, rest and give up the fast pace that she had been living. What a difference in her life.

In your own family, Human Design can change your life and theirs. I had to look at who I really was. I believed that chart because I really thought it was something specific for me and that I needed to learn to understand it when I was told that I was originally a Projector, not the Manifesting Generator from that one incident. Eventually

I just surrendered and decided, *"Okay, this is who I am."* The more that I worked with the energies of the Projector, the more I was convinced it is who I was designed to be. Now I really feel like that's the best thing because that's who I am. I still do a lot of things but I pace myself more in line with a Projector instead of Manifesting Generator.

I think when you with work with Human Design for a long time, you learn it just goes deeper and deeper and deeper. It's something that one continues to learn and grow from it is absolutely amazing to me. I know how I felt at when I first started studying I thought "it's going to take me forever to learn this because it's so deep." But I stopped worrying about that and just started doing it. The more you do it the clearer the understanding becomes. Human design to me is the way that I live my life. Something that my closest friends all know about and they all want to know more.

Figure 11. Linda Bissin Copp

Linda Bissin Copp is a managing family therapist, in practice for more than thirty years. A friend of nearly four decades introduced her to Human Design, which enabled her to understand her own family dynamics as a child in addition to events in her current life. Human Design brings efficiencies in her therapy practice for her clients and helped her understand the intricacies of her six children.

Linda has extensive credentials in the Human Design field and beyond, which compliment her counseling and coaching sessions. Her expertise includes: Human Design Level Four Specialist (nine years), Reiki Master Teacher (sixteen years), Level Four Aura-Soma Practitioner (sixteen years), Quantum Touch (twelve years) and a Meditation and Visualization Teacher. She is also certified in clinical hypnotherapy for specialty regressions since 1983, Re-Connective Healing for over thirteen years and a Mystery School Initiate.

She has studied with some wonderful teachers throughout the years, including Buckminster Fuller, Karen Curry, Peggy Bassett, Judith Reitz, Jean Houston, Kathryn Landers Vanvectin, Diane Schewmaker and many more. Linda has continued her search for truth throughout most of her adult life and will continue to follow her heart and spirit to guide her journey.

# Sandra Lee

# Facilitate

Can something determined by the positions of the planets impact the health of the physical body? As a skeptic about planetary influences, I never would have believed it. But now I do. Before learning about Human Design, I did not believe that the positions of the planets had any impact on me. Over the years, I had received astrology readings, but I remembered nothing about them. My experience was that astrology was irrelevant to my personal life. Other people may trust astrology to guide them in making critical decisions, but it just wasn't doing it for me.

My introduction to Human Design was on a teleseminar where a Human Design specialist was being interviewed. Nothing she said was addressed to me personally, yet I learned things about myself and my Design that are absolutely relevant to my everyday life and awareness. Surprised? You bet. I jumped with both feet into Human Design practitioner training and rapidly reached the status of Level 4 Human Design Specialist.

Although I remain a skeptic about the relevance of planetary positions, I am repeatedly astounded by how accurate this deceptively simple little triangle proves to be every time. I do readings for people who are complete strangers to me. Questions that I ask are drawn from their charts, not from our shared history. The responses that I hear repeatedly make it clear that the chart accurately describes their lives. These include, "Yes, I do that all the time," "That's me," "That makes sense" and perhaps most tellingly, "I wish I had known this twenty (or thirty) years ago."

Human Design tells you what themes will run consistently throughout the course of your lifetime. Your chart identifies particular gifts that you are likely to have. Awareness of your strengths enables you to most effectively strengthen and capitalize on them. It also reveals the potential challenges that you are likely to encounter. Armed with these insights into your personal makeup, you are able to look at difficulties from a new perspective and make empowering choices. I believe that the lessons you came here to learn show up through the circumstances that you attract.

Here is how I describe it: your Human Design chart is like a blueprint for your life. It draws to you people and circumstances that bring you opportunities to learn life lessons. Imagine that the triangle is invisibly laid over and merged with your energy body, becoming part of it. It beams out into the environment, calling out through the ethers to people who can offer these opportunities to learn and grow.

Relationships are your biggest, best school for life lessons. Whether people in your life make you angry or impatient, you feel you get blamed for everything or even if you feel exhausted or overwhelmed, the potential range of experiences you may have while in the presence of others is infinite. All of these experiences have specific energies in the Human Design chart.

Or perhaps it seems like *you* are the person who is always making *other* people upset, angry, impatient, or exhausted. It may be some aspect of how you are designed contributing to your being a disruptive influence on other people. Whichever side of this relationship dynamic you find yourself experiencing, you can now understand why it happens. There are strategies for how to make your experience of life more smooth, enjoyable and successful. That is what Human Design is all about.

For instance, imagine that you electromagnetically attract the very people who upset you, who set you off balance. Human Design describes a specific form of attraction called electromagnetics. Individual energies (or Gates) in your chart draw people to you who have complementary energies. These people are perfectly designed to provide you with incredibly valuable opportunities to learn and grow.

I have been hinting about potentially challenging ways that this attraction can look. Electromagnetics also attracts people who empower you and bring out your gifts. In fact, your personal trigger and your encourager can be embodied within the very same person! Someone who sets you off like a firecracker could simultaneously be the individual who can most support and empower you. The way that you choose to respond makes all the difference. When someone triggers your reactivity, you are at a potentially life-altering choice point. Though in the moment when you are upset, it may be difficult to recognize it as an opportunity. You could react and respond precisely as you habitually have or you can forge a new path. You can recognize what was happening and consciously decide to say or do something different. This is an incredible opportunity! When faced with adversity, you can choose to become a stronger person.

Year after year, you may have the same fight, the same difficulties with your spouse, child or parent — but the future of this relationship can change if you respond differently. Imagine how this shift in perspective could alter the quality of your relationship. Imagine how your life would transform. Consider giving thanks for the people who trigger you and the lessons they bring. Recognize that you actually attracted them. Isn't this a more empowering place to come from than remaining hot and bothered?

Choosing to find a new response might shift and transform your experience of this relationship from frustration to something closer to joy and love. At the very least, relating with this person might be easier, calmer and more peaceful for you.

*People are the vehicles that bring the treasures of life's lessons. This Is Your Personal Relationship School.*

You electromagnetically attract people who give you opportunities to contribute. Everyone is designed to make a unique contribution to the world, and your Human Design chart is like a roadmap to your gifts. It does not prescribe *what* you are designed to do. It describes general qualities that you are likely to express while engaged in contributing. Qualities like being creative, logical, intuitive, empowering, transformative and emotional.

Some people are designed to sustainably work for long hours, while other people become absolutely burned out by this sort of labor. Some people have to follow consistent routines to be able to function effectively, others do not. Some people are nurtured by working with animals or in natural environments. Other people thrive in body-centered occupations. The possibilities for contributing are endless.

Your Human Design chart is like a beacon, broadcasting to the world your talents. It beams out to draw in customers for your business. If you are a musician or an artist, your chart attracts people with opportunities to express your artistic gifts. The chart attracts the perfect people to satisfy whatever needs that you have and it also attracts the perfect people who need what you have to offer. When you live consistently with your design, it all comes to you. How amazing is that?

Here's a hint to post on the fridge, even if you remember nothing from the rest of this chapter:

*Your greatest gifts and your most frustrating challenges are frequently two aspects of the same energy.*

When you are experiencing difficulties, you can turn the coin over and choose, with intention, the positive aspect of that challenging energy. You can choose empowerment rather than remaining stuck in the negative.

Imagine what a difference it would have made to learn about your gifts and challenges during childhood! Your choices may have been different. (Here's a hint for parents. If you have children or know people who have children, Human Design readings are an incredibly valuable tool for knowing how to raise and support them.)

As you learn how to effectively handle the things that you struggle with most, you are developing valuable life skills and gaining tremendous wisdom. Once you master these areas of life experience, you have a treasure trove of wisdom that can benefit other people.

*Transform your struggles into your teachings.*

I love helping people understand themselves and their lives with the assistance of the incredibly powerful lens of Human Design. Identifying your strengths supports you in maximizing them. And identifying your potential rough spots enables you to discover ways to travel life's path with greater ease and grace.

Let me illustrate this with lessons I have learned about my own Human Design chart. I am a Manifestor. As a Manifestor, Anger is the emotional theme that runs throughout my life. This gives a variety of insights for my own Design.

**My Problem:** I get mad at the stupidest little things, like my husband putting things away in the "wrong" places in the kitchen. I used to give myself a really hard time about the anger. But I never seemed to be able to turn it off or make it go away.

**Resolution of My Problem:** Learning that anger will always be a normal part of my daily experience enabled me to become peaceful about this aspect of myself.

**Problem Management:** Now I recognize that I'm angry, communicate this if necessary, and just get over it.

The take home lesson is that if there are ways in which you judge yourself, learning that you are *designed* to have this experience enables you to become peaceful about these aspects of yourself. You can then come up with ways to manage these occurrences.

Another example from my own chart is that a central theme is Truth and Integrity or the Absence of Truth and Integrity. I recognize this as being the lens through which I experience everything in life. This means I am really good at finding the best, most efficient way of doing things. I'm terrific at finding errors and correcting them. When doing healing work, I assist people in having more truth and integrity in both their bodies and their life experiences. The gift of the lens of truth shows up everywhere and I'm incredibly grateful for it.

With Human Design, this gift helps me identify what my clients would most benefit from hearing about their charts. When they are having problems in their relationships or other life circumstances, the lens of truth gives me insight into strategies that may assist them in experiencing more truth and integrity within their situations. However, it also causes a problem, because it really bothers me when people are doing things in ways that I perceive as being "wrong," inefficient or harmful. This includes petty things like my husband putting dishes in the wrong cupboard.

I am a perfectionist. No one can do things perfectly, including me. I am forever dissatisfied with what people do, from my husband to my friends. And the person who I am hardest on is myself. This leads to other interesting issues for me.

**Gift and Problem Combined:** Frequently I see ways that the government's actions aren't exactly improving the health and quality of life of the people, of the environment or of the world as a whole. Is this a gift or a curse?

**Resolution of my Gift and Problem:** I recognize that my truth and integrity filter has been triggered. Something is out of alignment with my personal standards.

**Problem Management:** I choose an empowering way to address the situation. When an issue really needs to be addressed, communication can be extraordinarily helpful. Frequently, the most appropriate approach is to just let it go. If the circumstance is trivial, or if the situation is outside of my control, then letting go is often best.

Here is how this looks with my husband and the dishes. Occasionally, my exasperation has built up and I mention it to him. Most of the time, I recognize that he is doing the best he can, that dish placement is trivial and I give up being upset. This has become kind of a joking issue between us.

When it comes to perfectionism getting in my way, I have to deal with this each and every day. Though at times it is paralyzing, I consciously choose to relax my unreasonable standards for myself; otherwise, it would be virtually impossible to get anything done. This results in my own take-home lesson, that every energy in the Human Design chart can be expressed in both positive and not-so-positive ways. If you are in a challenging situation, turn the coin over and look for ways to choose positive aspects of the energy.

Say a project isn't working out and you're experiencing frustration. (This is something that people of any of the five Human Design Types can experience, and it is a particularly common feature of the Generator/Manifesting Generator life path.) Is there a difference between remaining paralyzed and stuck for four hours and getting yourself out of the mud in one hour? Absolutely. You can actively choose to flip yourself from being stuck in a disempowering mental space into a more empowering perspective. Other alternatives are looking for a new way of accomplishing your task or choosing to feel grateful for this opportunity to learn a valuable lesson.

When you are stuck, in effect you are moving *backward*. Stress and negative emotions are detrimental to both your health and happiness. Persistent stress is proven to contribute to *all* chronic health conditions. When you are stuck in negativity, there is also the potential for you to actually undo whatever forward progress you have made toward your goal. When angry or frustrated, I used to bang things around and physically damage objects around me. I could remain angry for *weeks* at a time. (How ridiculous is that?) When you are mired in a negative place, choose to come from a new, more positive mind space. Shift from moving backward to making forward progress.

It is quite possible that you will not be successful in accomplishing this quickly. Please know that whenever you are able to reach a more positive mental place, it is completely to your benefit. The capacity to make this shift in the moment requires skill. Developing it takes time and practice. When it comes to Human Design, everyone has times when they are living inconsistently with their truth. I certainly do. When you are not living by Design, in effect you are not expressing your truth — and it is a very common symptom that causes people to struggle. I believe the accumulation in the body of years of withheld self expression can lead to pain and other very common physical symptoms."

As a long-time practitioner of bodywork, I definitely recognize the connection between people's physical symptoms and their patterns of not living the truth of who they are. I believe that unresolved emotional traumas and energies store in the tissues of the body. I work to assist people in releasing this emotional content. I verbally cue them to be aware of this connection and to allow the stored energy to flow out of the symptomatic area.

Let me illustrate this connection with my personal experience. I clearly see that my design shows up as a pattern of behavior and a set of symptoms in my physical body. If you participate in the personal growth culture, you have probably heard the recommendation, "Decide what you want, and just go do it."

In Human Design, this is called Initiating, the ability to come up with an idea and just make it happen. However, only eight percent of the population are Manifestors, the Human Design Type that is designed to initiate. The blanket "just go do it" that is recommended for everyone may repeatedly lead you down a road of unbearable frustration and anxiety. If you are exasperated by seeming failures in successfully initiating and following through on your goals, then have hope. You can learn about your Human Design Type and the way that you are designed to make decisions and take action.

I actually am a Manifestor, so I am designed to initiate. But I also have aspects in my chart that make me sensitive to criticism, correction and rejection. I take them very personally. So rather than initiating, frequently I feel compelled to hold back. Now that I understand about being a Manifestor, I am conscious of ways in which I could be initiating. But I don't.

As a long-time practitioner of bodywork and energy work, I have learned to think of the shoulders, arms and hands as energetically representing how we express the truth of who we are, how we express our hearts. Much of how we contribute to people and to the world is through the actions that we execute using our arms and hands. I share the love I feel by using my hands to do things for people. I contribute my wisdom to others by using my hands to type on a computer the information that I desire to share.

How does holding back from making a contribution look in my body? My right shoulder is always tight. If I pay attention to it, I can feel that there is more tension in my whole right arm compared to the left. Every minute of every day, even when I consciously choose to relax, tension is there. The energy of reaching out and giving gets pulled back into my body. I hold the energy back, sticking it in my shoulder and neck, leading to neck and shoulder tension and even headaches.

I look at symptoms as being the soul's way of getting my attention. Is God or a higher power tapping me on the shoulder? With Human Design, you can prevent or resolve a serious health issue by becoming aware of choices that you should be making and actions that you should be taking. If you have physical symptoms, maybe you are living out of alignment with the truth of who you are, and that contributes to your symptoms. Fortunately, Human Design charts show the sorts of choices and actions that are individually most suitable for each person. It is not prescriptive and "do this" but more like "head in this direction" and "this is how it may look."

Someone I know has transformed her experience of life with the assistance of the combination of Human Design and the form of deep tissue bodywork that I practice. Working with her powerfully demonstrates to me how living by design makes a tremendous difference. Donna's first Human Design reading will be forever remembered as a turning point in her life. It made sense of everything in her life experience. She gained an incredibly powerful tool for understanding her relationships and the ways in which she responds to her day-to-day circumstances and interactions.

She jumped into learning about Human Design, soaking it up like a sponge. I continue to be inspired by her example. Donna deepens my understanding of Human Design each time that I hear about the realizations that are most current for her. She had tension throughout her body, particularly around the right neck, shoulder, arm and hand and the left hip and back. We began doing deep tissue bodywork, and she experienced relief from the tension and pain, but the relief didn't last.

We transitioned into doing Soma Neuromuscular Integration® (SNI), the comprehensive, eleven-session deep tissue integrative work that I have practiced since 1993. It assists people in releasing the accumulation of holding, distortion, and injury patterns that lead to symptoms. When your body is imbalanced and in pain, it is difficult to be the person you want to be in the world. When you release those accumulated patterns from the body and re-establish a more balanced state, a tremendous lightness and ease becomes available. The experience of going through SNI frequently provides people with space and freedom to step more fully into their true selves.

Donna completed SNI over the course of a couple of months. She released a tremendous amount of holding and tension that had accumulated in her body. In effect, her body had become the storage place for the energies of her emotions and unresolved experiences. Survival patterns she had developed of holding back her self-expression were visibly present in how she carried her body. As the holding patterns dropped away, the transformation became obvious, both experientially and visually.

While Donna's story shows her holding back of self-expression and the resultant storage within her body of emotional energies and of traumas, it's important to know that everyone does this! When you notice yourself holding back, how do you feel? I encourage you to notice how your body feels when this occurs. Take note of sensations you feel, such as tension, pain and numbness. Yet equally important to bring to awareness are your emotions. Begin to realize that your emotional state and the energies of the circumstances may actually be stored — by you — in the physical tissues of your body. If you have pain in your back, have knee problems, or experience headaches, you may be able to learn what is really behind them.

The understandings Donna gained through Human Design led to the recognition of the patterns that she had adopted to survive the stresses of her life and relationships. I facilitated a turning point for Donna, and she brought one for me. I am forever grateful for her presence in my life, and for her friendship.

"Sandra introduced me to Human Design, which started me on a journey of deep reflection, self-assessment, and personal change. Simultaneously, I committed to completing SOMA bodywork with Sandra. She is a master of body mechanics, as well as energy mechanics. The combination of Human Design and SOMA bodywork created one of the most powerful transformative experiences of my life. The changes in my inner life were reflected in my body. Learning to live according to my design lowers my resistance and results in a body free of pain." ~ Donna

Have you identified ways of being that are inconsistent with the truth of who you are? Do you think these may be contributing to physical or non-physical issues and symptoms?

When you recognize that your actions are inconsistent with your personal truths, you are then able to make choices in the moment that are more in alignment for you. Recall what I said about gifts, challenges and lessons when discussing my own chart.

*Flipping the coin when faced with challenges leads to lessons and gifts! Heading in the direction of expressing those gifts leads toward the path of full self-expression, fulfillment, and improved health.*

Everything in this chapter can only be seen in a general way when considering your own life. Examining your personal Human Design chart may reveal keys to understanding how your life experience and your health may be impacted by your beliefs, patterns, history, and more. When doing Human Design readings, there are several things that I like to emphasize.

- Making things about your Design easy for you to understand and relate to.
- Providing ways for you to see your Design in action in your daily life.
- Helping you understand why challenging experiences are happening. This helps you stop judging yourself about them and frees you up to feel more peaceful and move forward.
- Providing practical strategies for how you can approach the challenging circumstances in your life and your relationships.
- Helping you have more satisfying, fulfilling, and loving relationships.
- Seeing consistent themes that run throughout your life.
- Discovering how you can strengthen and more fully express your gifts.
- Identifying and becoming consistent with your life purpose.
- Empowering you to live the truths that touch and nourish your soul.

A final note about medical conditions... Please be aware that seeing a significant change in body issues and symptoms may take some time. You have reinforced patterns that resulted in these issues over the course of your lifetime. Unless you experienced an accident or another form of physical trauma or insult, the manifestation of physical symptoms required repeated programming over the course of years. If you have a physical or non-physical medically diagnosable condition, it is possible to shift it in positive ways. Be patient with your progress. Your body has a lot to unlearn and repattern into supportive strategies!

Figure 12. Sandra Lee

Sandra Lee has been a practitioner of bodywork and intuitively guided energy work for over twenty years. She trained with Karen Curry as a Level Four Human Design Specialist and Family Coach over a two-year period. Sandra also has a degree in chemistry, which is very unusual in the Human Design world.

As a health care provider and closet scientist, Sandra is fascinated by the impact on health of living by design (and of NOT living by design). What healing is available when your thoughts, life and body are in alignment with Both of your blueprints? Sandra truly believes that living in accordance with your Human Design blueprint certainly helps in optimizing the expression of your original DNA blueprint.

Sandra offers a program for people desiring to heal pain and other physical issues, restoring their bodies to higher levels of functionality.

# Section 3
# The Human Design Puzzle

# Lorie Speciale

# Puzzle Peace-ing

Life is like a multi-dimensional puzzle, filled with snapshots of picture pieces that overlap and intertwine. Some of the images are beautiful, some are not. Many of them are filled with color while others are black and white. Sometimes it takes a lifetime before all the pieces come together in a way that allows us to see with clarity the full, beautiful, magnificent picture of the story of our life.

My life has been quite a journey with many put-together pieces. Like most people, the pictures I created brought me a wide range of experiences with emotions from happiness and pleasure to the pain of grief and loss. I noticed even at a young age that I felt and thought differently than the people around me. I experienced a great deal of fear but always questioned the status quo. I quickly learned it was best to hold back the urge to share my thoughts and questions with others. I was intrigued by mystery and fascinated with intuition. For as long as I can remember, I've been on a quest to better understand what is seen and what is unseen as I look at this master puzzle called life: the big picture and the pieces.

When I was a young girl, jigsaw puzzles were very popular. You looked at the pictures on the box and bought the one you wanted to make. I learned the easiest way to put it together was by sorting colors and patterns. You looked for all the shapes with straight surfaces; the four corners were the easiest to identify. Putting all the edges of the puzzle together framed the picture and created a two-dimensional, flat container into which all the other pieces went. You already knew what the picture was going to look like, and this process brought clarity about the boundaries and the direction; you worked from the outside moving to the inside pieces.

When I was growing up, life was just like that in the 1950s where you would start things on the outside. Parenting, though undergoing a major shift at that time, was still strongly influenced by earlier expert recommendations of rigidity and sterility with warnings against being overly affectionate. Parenting meant molding through scolding and punishment. A parent's job was to enforce the rules and make sure their children conformed to what society wanted so they could fit. The expectation for children was, "Do as you are told!"

This process was in the air that everyone breathed, in the food they ate and the drinks they consumed all to ease the pain of such harshness. Children were often forced into shapes that were not a match. Many of these children were trapped in bodies and lives that did not fit them. Some learned how to move within the constraints, some broke down, and some are spending a lifetime breaking free!

No one is to blame. It was the expectation in the collective consciousness of the times. Now, theories expand our understanding beyond the boundaries once rigidly held as truth and we continue to evolve way beyond two-dimensional thinking. After all, we now all know and agree with certainty that the Earth is not flat and that people are breaking free from rigid containers (such as stereotypes).

I've always strongly disliked labels. Those two-dimensional flat shapes others try to force onto people so that they can see a familiar picture that reflects their beliefs and helps them determine their next move. I always knew something was "off" with the pictures defined by right or wrong and good or bad. It never made sense to me. But, as a child of the fifties, the only girl outnumbered by three brothers and parents in survival mode, I felt trapped into hiding who I really was and how I felt because children were seen and not heard.

When I tried to speak, I was called too sensitive. I didn't think anyone wanted to know what I had to say, so I learned to move within the constraints, conforming the best way I could by trying to be a "good girl," one who followed the rules and became somewhat invisible. This helped to keep my underlying rebellious nature squashed beneath my fear for survival. Yet, this force deep within me kept my Soul tethered to the Earth and the Divine. I remember lying on the ground with the scent of the earth and sweet grass all around me, looking up between the clouds into the endless sky and contemplating eternity. I wanted to understand infinity — way too expansive for my young brain to grasp, yet somehow I knew I was a child that belonged to the universe. Today, I feel blessed to be guided on my journey by Spirit who continuously offers me the next piece that leads me to the expanded and inclusive picture I glimpsed as a young girl.

I've received the guidance I needed at each juncture along the path of the journey of life, even though at the time I didn't always realize it or understand its value. With this guidance, I was able to move through many struggles, some of which have been shocking (such as divorce with an infant and two young children 36 years ago, as well as the catastrophic car accident of my youngest child six years ago). My love for my family and strong desire for health and healing has helped me push through many fears (which at times felt paralyzing), deal with life circumstances, and adapt. There have been many unforeseen and surprising twists and turns as I move to seek clarity about this "puzzle called life." I'm trying to determine which pieces are important to bring forward and what needs to be put into the background. I have truly been blessed with the inner strength and outer support to be able to turn my challenges into opportunities through my connection to Spirit and all the love I've given and received.

Like most people, I had been heavily conditioned by my environment and the way others reacted/responded to me. I developed beliefs about myself that became the boundary that I used to frame the picture of my world. I unconsciously searched for cornerstone beliefs and the flat edges of rigid data to build a picture that was familiar. For many years, I was not aware of the separation between who I really was and what I came to see and believe. It's important to remember that this began at an early age, so I had a lifetime of gathering evidence to build pictures that supported beliefs that came from the conditions I was born into and not the fullness of who I really am.

I believed that if I followed the rules and corrected the mistakes my parents made, I'd have a happy family life (I was so hungry for this). I recall one day sitting on my couch as I looked at the pictures that contained many of the pieces I wanted: a husband, children, a dog and our own home. I remember telling myself, "I must be happy because I have what I always wanted." This contract I made with myself and the picture it created all fell apart when my husband up and left me and my children.

As a single parent responsible for raising my three children by myself, I had to make many important decisions, one of which was how to support my family. I went back to school so that I could have a career that could make that possible. I loved science and math and chose the traditional field of physical therapy. After working a short time in a school for children with disabilities, I quickly discovered that to be more effective I needed additional education.

I am a born helper with a passion for learning. I've been guided to study many traditional and alternative healing methods that have informed my work and have led me down important life-changing paths of body/mind studies including psychotherapy and somatic therapies. I learned that my body is the home of my mind, emotions, spirit, and is also a source of great wisdom. All of what I experienced and learned helped me begin changing the direction of living my life from the "outside-in" to the "inside-out."

Through my health and healing journey, both personal and professional, I was able to find many missing puzzle pieces, yet so much about life was still a mystery. Why were we all so different with such different lives, desires, motivations and outcomes? There were still so many pieces that I didn't understand about myself, my family and others. Then, I met Human Design and it forever changed my life and ignited my world. Human Design shook up all the pieces to the puzzle and is helping me create a whole new picture with much greater depth, complexity, inclusivity, clarity and hope. It offers the big picture story about the evolution of humanity as well as each individual. Human Design has been a pivotal piece that is helping me to further shift to "inside-out" living, offering me a fuller sense of Self, solid ground and an expansive view of life.

Modern technology has opened up a world of opportunity for learning in a variety of ways and, for me, helps close the gap between science and spirituality. As a lifelong learner, I enjoy listening to a variety of classes offered through the internet, which is how I found Human Design. A Human Design specialist was giving a free telecast on an introduction to Human Design and I was fascinated. I loved the inclusive system that synthesizes ancient wisdom with modern knowledge, thus bringing together science and spirituality. Human Design offered me a blueprint of my energy system so that I can actually see who I am in regard to the energy I consistently carry and where I am more vulnerable to conditioning.

It also helps me make sense of my world. I now understand who I am energetically and how I've organized my life as a result of my own unique design. I also understand others more, and why we are different in so many ways! I understand my attraction to Spirituality and how I was organically guided after my daughter's accident to focus on Love and develop a deeper, more conscious connection to God and my Self: a significant turning point in my spiritual development.

I have found so many missing pieces by studying Human Design. Everything that I wrote above, I now understand about myself such as: why I feel different from other people around me, how I sometimes feel paralyzed by so many fears and why, at times, I feel invisible. I grasp how I use my intrigue with mystery and intuition as well as my direct connection to Spirit and drive for growth and transformation. I'm aware of infinity, my underlying rebellious nature, my strong need for alone time as well as family time and my own sensitivity. I can feel "exhausted" at the end of the day because I've used my keen sense about other people. Most importantly, I accept my desire to help others by offering them knowledge and guidance through problem-solving.

All of these energetic aspects of my personality (and so much more) are represented in the Gates, Channels and Centers of my Human Design body graph chart. How I express these aspects is a result of the internal synergy of my energy as met and shaped by my external environment.

One powerful lesson came during a class in which the facilitator pointed out indicators of inadequacy in the Human Design body graph chart. I identified with all of the indicators and was sure they were in my chart. To my surprise, I only had one indicator. Then, I looked at my mother's chart and she had all of them. This picture I believed about myself didn't even belong to me; it was my mother's energy that I was identifying, not my own. Knowing and understanding this is freeing me to let go of what isn't mine, step more fully into who "I am." I can form an important boundary between me and other people (as in this example, my mother).

Adding Human Design to my journey has been a freeing and exciting adventure that offers me greater love and direction in my life. Learning about what I call my Human Design Personal GPS, has helped me understand so much about my true Self. Similar to a car's GPS, it gives me a reliable, fail-proof way of making decisions that can get me from where I am in the present moment to where I want to go. The Personal GPS consists of one's guiding Authority, personality Type and Strategy.

There are five Personality types. Mine is a Projector — intuitive, sensitive teachers and guides who do not have sustainable energy.

I use to be very hard on myself with a great deal of critical self-talk and judgment. I always wondered why my energy level fluctuated so much. By the end of the day, I felt so tired that I'd fall asleep every night on the couch watching TV. I would do that even as a young mother, often before my children. Now I understand. I have compassion for myself where I use to have judgment and I seek to demonstrate greater self-care by giving myself what I need instead of depleting myself.

My guiding Authority, the place within my body I go for truth, is my Splenic Center. It offers intuitive guidance in the present moment. I have always been intrigued by intuition and think it's been greatly misunderstood. Intuition is woven throughout my Human Design Chart. It is my guiding Authority and prominent in my Incarnation Cross (my purpose). It's been so much fun to get to know this energy within me and very revealing. It's not as mysterious or "woo woo" as I once thought. For me, it's a frequency, like a radio or TV channel that in the past I simply didn't understand or know how to tune into.

My Strategy is that I need to wait to be invited. As I looked back through my life, I find that the major decisions I've made about school, career, relationships and even where to live came by the way of an invitation. Waiting can be challenging, but understanding that while I am waiting for those important invitations, doing more of what I enjoy (such as gardening, cooking, learning, creating, spending time with loved ones and being in nature) is essential to energetically create opportunities. This belief is way outside of the boundaries of the old flat two-dimensional puzzle or even the three-dimensional box that contained the puzzle! It creates a whole new somewhat magical and fun holographic motion picture.

I didn't realize before Human Design that as a Projector motivated to help others, I was often giving my energy away to people who were not asking for it or able to receive it. The result was I felt drained and this also made it more difficult for the people who wanted what I had to offer (were in a position to truly benefit from it) to find me. I understand why it's important to wait for the invitation and listen to my intuition for what to say. Now, my holding back is coming from a place of inner-wisdom instead of outer-conditioning. This makes it a very empowering experience instead of a disempowering one; it is a significantly important piece for me to have in the multidimensional puzzle of life. This simple, but not always easy, shift in perspective changed everything for me and is opening up amazing opportunities.

I use Human Design in every area of my personal and professional life. Not only do I understand myself from the inside out, I understand other people and how we all fit together. All of my relationships have benefitted. Understanding how we are all so energetically different has enhanced my communication with family, friends, coworkers and clients. Now when I feel the pressure to offer something I know or to do something, I can take a breath and remember that I don't have to solve the puzzle. I can trust that Spirit is providing what is needed when it's needed, and I can trust myself to know what my part in that is, by following my GPS.

This comes when working with all sorts of people, even little ones. I have a very tender place in my heart for children. Sharing what I know in a way that is supportive with all children (including my own children and grandchildren) is essential for me. I've worked with children with disabilities for thirty years, empowering them by creating the just right challenge. Learning about the five different personality Types and how each Type has a different Strategy for experiencing greater peace, success, satisfaction, and delight has been a gift. I weave this into my interactions with all children. This has been so rewarding as I see them integrate what they're learning into their lives. Teaching children how to use their Strategy early in life can be a very empowering tool for helping them identify what is true for them on the inside and decrease some of the external conditioning.

The time has come where there are more and more people in the collective to support a new generation of children who are being loved for who they truly are. Every person has a true self, a Soul that is a reflection of pure love. Every person has a right to be nurtured and supported so that this inner light of love can shine in and through them, from the "inside-out." Everyone has a purpose rooted in love and is needed by the world so that we can all know what pure love, peace, and happiness truly are even beyond our wildest dreams.

The journey from the "outside-in" to the "inside-out" is not an easy one. "Outside-in living" forces us to be who others want and expect us to be so that we can get the love and approval we need. "Inside-out living" frees us to *be* the love we are so that we can know happiness, share it with others and add more love to our world. This is a major paradigm shift and requires inner strength as well as outer support. I have discovered by observing my own personal transformation as well as those of people with whom I've worked that we are often further along our journey than we are even aware.

When I sit with another person, I am honored to be given the gift of seeing that beautiful magnificent person from the "inside-out." We are all on our own journey, and yet we were not designed to journey completely alone. We are social beings who need other people, and although that looks different for different people, as long as we are here on Earth we do need each other. When we understand our differences and realize that so much of what we took personally really isn't personal but rather reflects our different energetic needs, we can ease into greater acceptance of ourselves and others. As we continue to make room for our differences, it's helpful to remember that we are all innocent. There are no mistakes, only mistaken expectations.

At one time, I bought into believing that I was stuck with the pictures that were created by the way those pieces were handed down to me. Now, I know differently. The one resounding theme that reveals itself in every picture throughout my life (though it shows up differently) has been my connection to Spirit; the piece that brings me peace. My spirituality does not attach itself to any one particular religion. For me, God is Love. I am so grateful to know through my connection to Spirit that what might appear disempowering can be empowering and that fear can be transformed to faith through the eyes of Love. It is my wish that you come to know this, too!

The multidimensional puzzle of life is ever-expanding; it cannot be contained within the boundaries of our minds. We are not responsible for trying to put the whole puzzle together, only for doing our parts by living out the highest expression of the stories of our lives. I am learning to trust that we all have everything we need, and when something more is needed, it is given. So, we can all ease ourselves back into the secure embrace of mother earth, behold our loving universe and enjoy the multidimensional living-color motion picture that we all create together.

Figure 13. Lorie Speciale

As a gentle Intuitive Guide who listens with her body, mind and spirit, Lorie Speciale is committed to helping others connect to their true nature. She believes that using her expertise as a New York State Licensed Mental Health Counselor, a Certified Rubenfeld Synergist®, a Gestalt Therapist, Human Design Specialist, and Certified in EFT (Emotional Freedom Technique), she can help clients release conditioning in the body, mind, emotions and spirit that interrupts their natural flow and life force.

Driven by her own desire to move from fear to faith as a result of her own life challenges, Lorie has been highly motivated to extract, distil and integrate what she has learned from multiple therapies. In partnership, she can see and hold a sacred space, reflecting back the miracle that you truly are, connecting to what is really true *about* you and what is true *for* you, thus creating an opening in your life in which what you desire becomes possible.

She uses her love of learning to continue to expand her knowledge and experience. Lorie knows that it is possible to return to love and joy, no matter what struggles life brings. She is committed to helping others do that in their own lives as well thus adding more Love to our world.

# Dave Buck

## Playing

Have you started a business, sought a promotion or hunted for a soul mate, only to be slowed down or even derailed by unexpected struggles? You work hard. You get creative. You follow a blueprint. And the roadblocks keep coming. You double-down. You analyze and dig deep. But even after doing everything possible, nothing works. Why? It can't be you.

But it is.

It *is* you.

You were born a baby human with unique perspective, rare qualities, and even superpowers. At first, the people in your world are amazed by your every cute coo, celebrating your amazing individuality. But, when you get to be two or three, the celebration turns to criticism. You use the most powerful ways you know to express yourself — you cry and whine and swing your little fists and stomp your foot — but it does not work. Your superpowers annoy, alarm, and anger the big humans. They do not bring you more love or affection. So you adapt.

Every human being's identity is shaped by how they adapted to the expectations of their environment. We are adaptive creatures. Even when the root of an expectation or pressure is meant for our good, it can tamp down who we really are. Those raising you did not need to intend harm even while teaching you a lie.

For example, one imperative may be your safety. So let's say you're four years old, and you start lining up all your brothers and sisters — older *and* younger — in a line. And you tell them the order to move, where to stand, to stop picking their noses, to be quiet, and to listen to you. The adults in your life see this and call you "bossy." And if you are bossy, then that means you may not listen to them even if it is in your best interests... when it keeps you safe. To the adults, it makes perfect sense to say, "Hey, you're only a little four-year-old, so simmer down. You're not the leader around here. We're the leaders. Stay safe. We love you."

So you try to "simmer down." And you may not succeed all the time but you try because you trust the adults and you seek their approval and sense their love. So at only four years old, you learn to hide your inborn leadership ability. You begin to be quiet. You learn to make the adults feel better by hiding your most precious gifts, your strengths and superpowers. You also learn to hide where you are special because it could make you vulnerable to the world. You are not supposed to be vulnerable or special. You are four. You are cute. The adults in your life have made you safe inside your box. And so you learn not to be special.

A couple of years later, you are taught to sit in little rows at little desks and ordered to be quiet, listen, and do what you're told. Day after day and year after year, you learn to put yourself into that safe box. You do not grow out of it; you grow into it. You make it logical to stay in the box, an assumed part of Life. Maybe you question it when you are a teenager, but you quickly understand that anything outside the box is dangerous and unacceptable in society, by the people who can make life grand or hell.

The world *says,* "You be you!" But it taught you to live in the box, to *be* the box. Teaching you was not (usually) meant to be malicious or cruel; it was because the world used to work best that way. You were born into an industrial world where everyone was supposed to get a job, get married to The One, work hard, not ask questions and you'll be safe. This is the box in adulthood.

And to prepare for it, in school you were told to do things yourself, to "figure it out." It was cheating to use tools — a simple calculator, for example. Just do your own work. Do not ask for help, because that means you're weak. And definitely don't share with your neighbor, because that means you are a cheater... the worst crime you could commit. Helping the kid sitting next to you was frowned upon; asking for help, discouraged. So you learned and adapted to be a smart little human, to sit by yourself and do your own thing and don't ask anybody anything.

Fast forward. Now you are forty. You decided to go with the people who could make life wonderful and you have been slaving for years inside that box. But for whatever reason, you suddenly realize that your career is not fulfilling. You want a new career or to start a business, so you seek to explore and discover other worlds, broadening your horizons to see what you have never seen, to find your "thing."

So you begin to put your Self out there. But this self is so used to being a little box that things get really confusing. You try, but you are able to muster only a tiny fraction of who you were born to be. And though you begin to be aware of the box, you begin to break out; the world takes your efforts to become free and turns them into work.

You are seeking a fulfilling life. You are beginning to see the box, even beginning to break out of it, and those self-sufficient skills you were told would make your life grand are holding you back—because the industrial age crumbled. (Hang with me; it's not all bad news. Hope is coming.)

So you see, it is you. But it is not you. The world you were trained for has transformed. Jobs have not lasted. The One you married left you for a job. You work so hard, you're exhausted. You are drowning in questions and you are most definitely not feeling "safe."

All the rules you were told in childhood are gone and it's a whole new world. This new era is the connected age. You need to be connecting and collaborating and co-creating to be successful, but you were not trained for this... you were actually trained to *not* do it. So what do you do? You ditch work for *play*.

The problem is that we really stink at playing. We are awful at having fun! But we are great at work. A good friend of mine once said, "You're in a restaurant, eating a delicious meal, having this beautiful experience. And then the waiter comes over and says, 'Still working on that?' What? I'm not *working* on this meal. I am loving it. I'm enjoying it. I'm not working. And my friend was right. We turn everything into work. It's crazy.

Industrial babies were taught to never make mistakes or get wrong answers. You were taught that life is a job. You are here to do your work and 'work' on everything.

We work in our careers.

We work on our golf game.

We work on our relationships.

We work on our diet.

We work on our children.

We freakin' *work* on everything!

When we are born, we are expected to jump into life and start *working*, finding our way as we go, 'working on our weaknesses,' practicing until we perfect our strengths.

But this model no longer *works*.

The superpowers from the industrial age are now outmoded. To be recognized, seen and successful all require authenticity more than work-based skill.

But you were trained to be in and become the box. You were taught to mistrust your superpowers — remember that bossy little leader child who was told to be quiet? Now, the world has changed fundamentally. You have to be on Facebook or Twitter. You've got to express yourself, be vulnerable and share your unique qualities. You've even got to (ugh) "brand yourself." And you think, "Yikes, I was taught to *never* be real." Remember that wailing child?

To recover your original superpowers takes rigorous exploration of our gifts, strengths, and weaknesses. If you want to build a business or rise to a leadership position or even find the love of your life, all of these things require that you be seen and known for who you *really* are. It is the only way to be sure the connections you make are authentic. It is the only way to escape the box. Does this sound like work? Maybe it feels like it at first, but no; truly, it is not work.

It is not a job! It's a game!

As with most games, there are rules to follow that will help you win. This is how we can turn around what we've learned and go back to who we are. In this game of life, these rules are spelled out for you in your unique Human Design Player Card.

In the Game of Life, your Human Design chart is your player card.

When I saw my own chart, I was amazed. Everything I had forgotten became clear. Right there in front of me, I could see what I was here to do. I started thinking back to when I was a child. I was always creating games. But at school, they said, "We don't play games. We do worksheets." So my creative instinct got squashed. When I first saw the Human Design chart and system, someone told me, "Dave, you're here to be the game player of life." The light dawned as I realized that I was here to play and help others play.

Sometimes games can seem very serious. And sure, this one is serious, because this is Life we're talking about. But I would call it serious *play*.

What do you do when you find out you are in the wrong game? Or an unwinnable game? Your player card will show you how to play the game of life to your best advantage. The coolest part is that when you play to your advantage, it helps those around you play to their best advantage, too. It is never competitive. It is collaborative.

Your role in this game of life has a persona and superpowers, strengths, and vulnerabilities. You are born as a player, not a worker. You were born with a Human Design chart, with a player card.

To win the game of life means to live your purpose—what you are here to do—on your own terms. If for example, you are trapped in a job that does not utilize your superpowers or actually wants you to suppress them, then you can't win there. So in order to not become trapped, you must know your superpowers. There are 36 superpowers in the Human Design system. Some people have one; some have several. When you know which ones you have, then you can find a way to create your own game of life.

It usually takes a while to create your game, requiring you to keep taking steps in that game's direction. Before you can create your own game of life, you must take the first step and discover who you were born to be. How? You look at your Human Players chart to find your superpowers.

Let's look at my player card to see how it all works. This part of the system is based on 36 superpowers. In my influence area, it says I'm here to create drive. I motivate people, especially in how to fight for their own freedom and how to play their life as a game. That's my unique quality, what I'm here to share with the world. I am a driver, with great ambition. Some people have a lot of ambition; some people don't. Nothing wrong with either way.

So, each superpower has nuance, as well. My drive has two meanings. One is the fight for individual freedom. I am ready to help individuals to be free. So if someone is stuck or trapped, I'm on it. The other aspect of my drive is the "game player of life." I am actually here to show people to play the game of life! I was born to do this!

And just like I get jazzed about learning my own superpowers, I have watched so many people become just as excited and amazed as they learn why they are really here, what they are born to do.

My card also has a lot of white space, indicating vulnerability. The key to vulnerability is that it is where you want to learn from the world and where you take the world into you. And the superpower that has always compelled me in my vulnerability is in the throat area, which I've always called "finding your voice."

My vulnerability is that I don't have a well-defined voice. It is always shifting and changing. If I hang around someone for more than two days, I start talking like him or her. I pick up accents when I travel and have always unconsciously used people's expressions. Now I understand that it is because that's how I am designed. It is a superpower even when it is a vulnerability. That's my superpower. My throat is wide open.

And this is really good to know. I don't have to "freak out" when I sound like people because that's what I do, and understanding this about myself is comforting. And because it is a superpower, it is not only a vulnerability, it is one of my main questions for the world. What is your voice? What are you here to express? I ask that question of the world. I don't have the answers. I only have lifelong questions.

In my own way, I help people look at their player card and figure out which of their superpowers on which they should focus. There is just so much information for you in this player card. You learn where you are vulnerable from the Centers, where you are open versus closed, how you learn from life, but also how you could be manipulated by life. Often you learn where you're trying to be something that you're not supposed to be, that you are not born to be.

When you learn where you have adapted in a way that is not true to your core, it can be very illuminating because the universe never lies. If you are struggling, it is probably because you have adapted and tried to be something that's not true for you, not the real you.

Let's say you have a dream to become a singer. You feel born to sing, you are great at singing, you have a drive to sing, but you're struggling. You comfort yourself by saying that not everybody is meant to be a top 40 star or opera singer. You keep struggling, trying everything you know to make it work but feel like you are just spinning your wheels.

Human Design can help. If you look at your superpowers on your player card, you might discover that you are singing songs not true to your core self. Maybe you realize you have been trying to force your way through success by singing what you think others want instead of what you are supposed to be singing, and that's why your songs are not resonating with people. It is not that you lack talent. But there are many super successful singers with terrible voices. And many great singers never made it. It is most likely because they're singing to please instead of singing with their true voice songs they're here to sing.

Those of us who grew up in the industrial age learned to hide our real selves and our superpowers so deeply that we don't even know we're doing it. No matter what you're trying to do, if you get to the core of who you are born to be — getting clear about that, you will have much more success. One way or another, you will meet success when you align with the design of your life, even finding success in your vulnerable areas.

Once you have discovered your superpowers, the next step is to figure out what kind of game can you play. This is a lifelong goal, but it starts today, with even incremental movement. You sneak your superpowers into your job a little, get a slightly different job, or maybe you take up a hobby. Once you discover who you are born to be, it becomes real; you will find a way to bring it into the world.

It is hard to be full of wonder like and childlike. Looking at a common family situation with two siblings, sometimes one is so fulfilled while the other is struggling. After digging into it, we discover that one was born when the family was happy and one was born after the dad lost his job. These siblings grew up in two different environments even though it was the same house. Siblings are going to adapt and respond to their surroundings in different ways. The one under stress is most likely to squash any superpowers that might increase the stress. The one who formed early response patterns when the family was stable is more likely to know and use any superpowers fully and without fear.

Once you begin to understand the context and pressures that influenced your early superpower development, you are better equipped to make different choices. You unravel what you've learned that may or may not be serving you, ultimately starting to choose what supports who you are meant to be in this world. You do that by creating an environment that actually nourishes and embraces being yourself rather than trying to squash it and to be like everybody else.

When we start understanding these forces and begin to change, it can get really hard due to one word: shame. In that early childhood training, we learned to hide our true selves and then go even deeper, learning to fear your superpowers. When fear and shame are part of teaching, it takes immense and profound courage to explore and bring our superpowers out into the world.

A coach or guide — like this book — can help. You are not alone. Contrary to what we are taught, this is not a do-it-yourself life. Don't play this game alone. Be alert and humble enough to find and accept guidance and help. Here's why:

When fear and shame suppress our superpowers, it impacts even the process of becoming free. As you learn about human design, your player card, and begin to choose for your true life, fear as well as shame can derail your intentions and efforts with powerful, ingrained doubts. You may think, "Who am I to do this?"

You may believe, "I'm not good enough" or "I don't have enough training." Perhaps you're concerned with, "I don't make enough money."

There are other worries we impose on ourselves, too. "I'm too fat." "I'm too thin." "I'm too old." "I'm too young." These thoughts detract from your glimpse of your true purpose. All the advice — free or exorbitant — in the world will not make it work.

"Be yourself." Right, that's only the hardest thing in the world to do, especially when fear and shame are at the root of hiding your real self. We are all trained to work alone and be terrified of each other, but we are taught that to be successful, we have to build relationships and it's a piece of cake. Just go do it. Just "add value." These are the three hardest things in the world. And they do not solve the problem and are even impossible to do unless we get to the core of ourselves and to the root of our fear and shame.

To live our best life and most authentic self, we have to become visible to ourselves first. Afterward, we can reveal ourselves to the world with no fear or shame.

The first step is to understand our superpowers, and your player card is your guide. Start by asking two big questions: Does my environment appreciate and support my superpowers? Is 'where I am' a place I can be my true self? That takes time to figure out and it's not an overnight process. It can be complex.

This is totally out of the comfort zone for those taught and trained to shut up and do what they are told, to not ask questions, heard that they are not that special and that uniqueness is a threat so be like everyone else. We really have to start elbowing our way out of that comfort zone so we can get to those bigger questions because we have learned our superpowers and are beginning to feel that we are worthy to be ourselves.

This happens far more often to whose over forty years old because we lived in the industrial revolution, which depended on training people to be like machines. As the industrial social structure has crumbled, is has been particularly difficult for those over forty to both realize that we really were born to be special and to not squash it (or see it as bad in the younger generation, either).

The newer generations can teach us. They have not been raised with the same fears. They are beginning their lives without the shame so when they go for what they want, they do so without the same kind of fear as older generations experience. It is not that younger generations want rewards without work or gain for nothing. It is that they are not as afraid, not as ashamed, and they're not willing up to give up their lives to slave under a structure that has crumbled.

They want life — even "work" — to be fun and playful. They have not lost their sense of play. They are here to play. In the old, industrial structure, that seems irresponsible and unrealistic. But the industrial lie finally crumbled, allowing us to see that humans are here to play. We need to get on board with them and play!

As you learn who you are, maybe at the beginning this might feel like work. And there are steps to it. But at its heart, it is play. You start with the foundational pieces. You do your Human Design chart and get your player card to discover your superpowers and find out who you were born to be. Trust the system. You start playing... not working. Remember, you are *playing* the game of your life. You can't control life, but you can influence it if you learn how to play.

Next, you start crafting an environment. If you are not in an environment that embraces who you were born to be, you find and build one. Facing more fears and stepping out of your comfort zone, it helps you learn your real life.

These things are all learnable, coachable. You can practice them. You can fail at them, get back up, and get better at them. Soon, you see that you're playing, and that becomes the game of your life: to keep getting better and better at being the real you in the world. You are here to play for real and to learn what is in your heart that is yearning to be freed.

There has got to be something that you really want. There are many catalysts to this: "I started a business, and I'm so excited but it's a struggle" or "I really want this promotion" or "I really want to find my soulmate." It takes courage to feel the pain, and we need to decide how we can elevate the true self.

The human spirit and the human survival instinct are always in a dance. I used to call it a fight, but now I call it a dance. On the one side, there is your human spirit. You are here to express something and be something in life that's always happening and it comes through your heart's desire and finds its way into your life.

On the other side is your pre-programmed need to survive life, that 50,000 years of human evolution of survival instinct. It knows that the way you survive is by fitting into your social group. So the human spirit and the human survival are always in this dance and sometimes the spirit ekes through while sometimes the survival overtakes it. This dance happens every day of our lives.

For example, when someone grows up in very difficult circumstances (abused, moving around, never valued), their spirit leaves. It happens to so many people. Their selfhood and superpowers are suppressed, and they learn that to survive. They usually don't do it consciously; it is unconscious; some rise and some fall.

It is a mysterious process how some rise and fall, but there are some clues. One is that if a person can get into a different environment in some way — even a very small way, where their natural gifts and superpowers are embraced and supported — then they can begin to thrive. The human spirit is tenacious and, like a weed in a sidewalk crack, will squeaking through with even the tiniest of nourishment. So the trick is to find, recognize, and build those environments and opportunities.

Once someone gets into an environment where his or her superpowers and gifts are an asset, then he or she will thrive. So once you have even just a little more of a conducive environment, and once you are willing to learn how to play, you are ready for the step. Let's look at the steps a little more closely.

Every human has a question for the world and there are three kinds of phases around that core.

The first is play. When you are "living at play," you are naturally using your gifts. When you are living at work, you are usually suppressing your gifts. You must find a way to play, tap into your gifts, express them, experiment, create and find safe spaces where you can do what you're here to do.

To bring joy where you are while you make changes externally, you can start with noticing your body. We are taught to ignore our body, camouflage pain by cutting it off, and pretend the body does not exist (even while it moves us around). We've got drugs for whatever pain is happening. Instead of the aspirins, antidepressants and caffeine, you say, "I'm here. As I'm awakening to the idea of my own energy and my own capacity to choose, I'm noticing this place I'm in doesn't feel good. I've been disguising my dissatisfaction with coffee, television and drugs for a long time."

Once you ease out of those things, most spiritual teachers start with getting you into your body, learning how to feel deeply... something that we do not learn in school. You can accomplish this by trying to eliminate as many camouflaging substances and experiences as you can, as gradually as necessary. Start to feel.

Inner freedom is our second phase, and it comes from understanding in addition to overcoming the fear of being your true self. We all learn to be afraid of our gifts because expressing and using them in our social environments often results in emotional and physical pain, trauma, and violence. But inner freedom is how to play with that fear.

Knowing your Human Design chart helps you begin to be able to play with fear. Dive into your player card. Get to know your gifts, your questions, your superpowers, where you express energy and how you receive energy. Get to know who you were before the fear took over.

Pay attention to resonance. It is a body experience, yes, but it's also a little bit in your mind. For example, when you're around a person, notice how you feel. You may be drawn to someone, or notice your energy changes. Decide to trust these feelings. Practice.

Creating Supportive Environments is the third step that really ties with the second phase. So often, we are taught to ignore our environment and consider it to be set in stone. We think of it as a wholly external, uncontrollable force and blame it for what goes wrong in our lives. "I hate my job." "This is the wrong location." "I just have to quit." "I can't quit because I have three kids and have to pay the bills."

We can't always control our environment. The key is to learn how to find and create an environment that draws out and accentuate your gifts, superpowers and core questions—it's where your gifts are maximized rather than squelched, dismissed or ignored.

It's an ongoing process, and every situation is unique. One method is to start with the assumption that wherever you are, you're there for a reason. Every environment is made up of people, places, things and ideas. A safe supportive environment is where you can fully express yourself without fear in all those ways.

The most important ingredient (by far) is people. The game is played best when you find people who love you when you are being wholly yourself. It has to do with that resonance you began to notice when building inner freedom. You begin to pay attention to how it feels when you click with someone. You notice that whenever you're around this person, the sparks are amazing. Ideas flow and it's exciting and you want to do stuff together.

You choose to spend time with people who feel like that more often than not. You must find your tribe, your "peeps." Human Design especially helps with this step, because learning about interacting with others usually involves people who are also getting to know their charts. So you can look at your two charts and see how you might click for one reason and not another.

In these three phases, Human Design is a really good tool because it gives you good clues. If you feel an energetic connection with someone, then you ask for their birthday. When you look at the charts, you can usually immediately see why things click. You'll be able to identify the places on your charts where energies connect, gifts match and superpowers are synergistic. Most importantly, trust your body in recognizing authentic connections with others.

In history, people were born into your community and you stayed with that group from the day you were born until the day you died. You had no choice but to adapt to these humans. No choice. In the modern era, most humans have at least a little more choice and many have far more leeway to choose our community, our home. In the context of human evolution, we have no practice making these choices. We are wired to behave as though we have no choice.

But now, we can live just about anywhere in the world. Most of us have some choice of career, community, language and passion. Now that we have this freedom, we have to learn how to use it powerfully. We must learn to choose people we really click with, no matter where they are in the world or how we meet them. Once you build your little posse, your life really starts to hum, because they are the people that energize you.

That magic is from the people and environment—mentally, emotionally, and physically, too. You've got your tribe, and then you start noticing every physical space has energy. Some make you feel really alive and other physical spaces make you feel like you have to get out before it kills you. You become attuned, learning your body, learning to notice where feels really good. Your goal is to organize everything around you for what feels great.

We can break the chain from the past, where choices and feelings did not matter. If you are in a place that doesn't feel good, leave. If you are in a job and the office makes you depressed, quit (and find another place). Learn to trust your energy about people, places, things and ideas. Keep choosing and choosing and choosing, upgrade, take little steps; keep making it a little better.

Choosing the thing that feels better and good becomes your operating principle as you start playing in this environment that energizes you. You experiment, risk, try new things and learn from everything. That is how to play all the time. Experiment, play, learn. Deal with your fear, notice your fear, understand your fear. And you shift from fear to wonder.

Wherever you are, you look for the reason you're there. When you start with certainties and with real authenticity, you will quickly determine sometimes you have learned everything you can. Then you start actively seeking what's next. So much is possible as you learn from "where you are" and then gradually shift where you put your energy next.

You will shift from survival to choice even faster if you have a coach, helping you discern and learn from all that risk. When you have another person helping you, they can help preserve the sense of play and increase understanding. You are not alone. My own coach, Thomas Leonard (who I think is the original life coach of the world), always used to say this really profound thing to me: "The universe never lies."

He meant that if you want to go out in the world to build a business or get promoted or find the love of your life and it's not happening or it's a big struggle... that's the universe telling you something is askew. So rather than continuing to struggle and focusing on what is not happening, step back. Acknowledge that the universe is telling you to stop and take a time out. Look in a new direction.

Often, the direction you need to look is within you. Your player card, your Human Design chart, is one really effective tool to use to do that.

And here's the really provocative truth: as a human being, you are going to continue to adapt to your environment until your last day. Adapting is not wrong. When you choose (friends, coworkers, even what you read), you choose what you will inevitably and naturally obtain. You can actually craft who you want to become in the world by choosing who you hang around, where you go and what you do. You keep choosing new possibilities for yourself by choosing new people.

It is all about choosing. As we begin to create who we want to be in this world, do two things: connect with people who share your purposes and tune into who you were born to be. Continue to do this with such clarity that you effortlessly craft the environment that is a reflection of who you were born to be, so you can become who you choose to be, playing the game with truth and authenticity.

Peace everyone. Play your life.

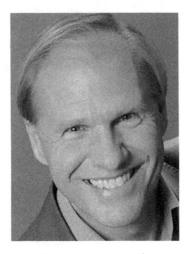

Figure 14. Dave Buck

Coach Dave Buck is an MBA, Master Certified Coach and the CEO of CoachVille, the original global online community for Coaches with over 36,000 members in over 70 Countries. Dave is a leading visionary voice of professional coaching. A 2008 independent global survey of 10,000 professional coaches named Dave the seventh most influential person in the history of professional coaching. Dave is on a quest to teach leaders how to transform from 20th Century Management Science to 21st Century Coach Approach Leadership.

Dave is a spiritual adventurer with a love of personal growth and world travel. He lived in Bolivia for two summers on a quest to LIVE the game of soccer. He has also traveled through Southern India with a Tamil Siddha on a quest to learn how to compress time.

Prior to becoming a Professional Leadership-Life Coach, Dave combined his BS in Computer Science with his MBA to design and implement business information systems for several Financial Organizations including AT&T Capital (now part of GE Capital) and First Sierra Financial (now part of American Express). Dave has appeared on numerous television interview programs, radio shows and print publications including feature articles in Entrepreneur Magazine and Choice Magazine.

# Evelyn Levenson

# Welcome Home

Could I leave a dying man?

It was definitely a tough decision. I really didn't want to be married to him anymore, but I couldn't abandon him either. He had been diagnosed with AIDS several years before. He was still alive and doing okay… at that time. But there was nothing at all for me in the marriage—there hadn't been for the last five of our nine years married. And I just couldn't do it anymore.

Fortunately, we had managed to maintain an amazingly good relationship, given the circumstances. For that, I was very grateful. And incredibly, I consistently tested negative for HIV, for which I was (and still am) extraordinarily grateful.

Had I known then (1985) what I know now about myself, life, and relationships, I would have had a MUCH easier time understanding the personality and relationship dynamics at play and a MUCH easier time making the decision I eventually made. It could have been SO MUCH LESS PAINFUL than it was. *Why was I having such a hard time letting go? Why did I always bend over backward to please others (especially him) and care so much about what others thought of me? Why did I have such a hard time knowing who I was, what I wanted, and what I should do with my life?*

These and so many more questions were finally answered when I came to understand myself, the world, and others through Human Design. But I'm getting ahead of myself. I moved out that year and divorced him the following year. I paid him alimony, visited him often, and ensured he was taken care of until he passed in 1988.

During those years, I felt so relieved that I had found and put into place a more-or-less "elegant solution." It was a way that took care of me and supported my fledgling sense of "self" (not to mention my sanity) without abandoning him, which would have compromised my personal values and commitment. But I'd be lying if I told you it was an easy process.

Fast forward to several years later when I found myself struggling with a career decision. I was a really hard worker, smart and dedicated, yet I would burn out after about two years in a job and then would want to take some time off. I thought something was wrong with me; my peers didn't seem to have this problem. The bigger issue was that I really didn't know what I wanted to do next. I had enjoyed considerable success in the business world (and the federal government before that), but there was something missing. I knew I was capable of a far different contribution than my executive career track. I knew I wanted to be of service in a way that truly helped people at a deep level, but I had no idea how to do that.

I went through personality testing, career testing, aptitude testing, and a six-week career workshop. They were somewhat useful, but only gave me little pieces of the puzzle—not even enough to sense a direction to pursue. Despite having two Masters degrees, I was at a loss. One career counselor told me to leave behind my exceptional attention to detail because it wouldn't serve me as I moved up the corporate ladder. That was probably true, but I was proud of my attention to detail and it had always served me well. Ouch. Okay, now what?

I figured out that I didn't want to continue in the corporate world or the federal government. So I quit and took some time off. I was invited to become a partner in a small consulting firm and did that for about 10 years. Then I took some more time off. I looked into real estate investing. I learned about puts and calls in stock market investing. I dabbled with Quicken (accounting software) consulting as well as QuickBooks (business accounting software) bookkeeping and consulting. I took even more time off. Then I studied Health Coaching for a year. I knew I was getting closer, but I wasn't there yet.

Within weeks of me completing that coach training program in 2008, my mom entered the last stages of metastasized breast cancer. After being her full-time caregiver for her last five months, followed by sorting out the details of her estate (ever grateful for my attention to detail), I found myself peering at this weird-looking thing called a Human Design Chart that I had requested a few months earlier but hadn't had a chance to review until that moment.

The little bit I learned from the free report that came with my Chart was enough to rock my world. WOW. Suddenly, so much of my life that hadn't made any sense to me before made sense! It was like a veil had been lifted, and I saw with clarity why I was the way I was and how I fit into the bigger picture of life and humanity. I felt a tremendous sense of relief. The more I learned about myself through Human Design, the deeper that relief was and the more I realized that there was nothing wrong with me! It's just how I'm designed. There is nothing to fix.

I began studying Human Design for my own benefit, wanting to learn everything I could about myself. This is actually predictable from my Chart: I am a Projector with an open Identity Center and a 1/3 Profile—so I am investigative, probably don't have a clear direction in life, and have a hard time knowing what is true about myself. I also have STRUGGLE built into my Design. That explains a lot. Struggle in a Human Design Chart doesn't have to manifest with the everyday things (career, relationships, or self-definition). The purpose of Struggle in a Chart is to help a person find what is truly meaningful to them. I sure wish I had known that earlier.

As a Projector Type, I am here to guide the energies of others, not to do the "work" of the world. No wonder I was a "natural" at being a manager in my corporate and government careers. No wonder guiding students and doing intensive one-on-one work with clients feels so good to me. These are the highest and best use of my inherent energy configuration!

Knowing my Type has altered how I structure my business and my life. It finally allowed me to fully step into my guiding role without guilt or doubt. My Chart also shows that I am here to provide ideas and answers that restore the flow of energy, help others find meaning in their lives by sharing my own struggles as well as experiences, and move people into profound self-love and self-empowerment. I feel like a lucky girl.

The clarity created by learning all of these things had a life-changing impact on understanding my mission in life and guiding my business. Working with Human Design turns out to be the perfect vehicle for me to express my full Self. It is deeply rewarding to guide clients to "see" the truth and beauty of Who They Really Are, illuminate their blind spots, move through their energy blocks, and apply and integrate this profound knowledge into their lives.

Through the openness in my Chart (four Centers defined, five Centers undefined), I can feel clients' "a-ha" moments as they learn aspects of their energy and personality they didn't previously know. I delight in their "ahhh" moments of relief as they hear confirmation of what they "sort of" knew but weren't fully confident about understanding. Among other specific energies in my chart, these three are particularly useful in the work I now do: depth (Gate 48), logical arrangement of details (Gate 62), and storytelling (Gate 56). Having confidence that I experience and express these energies consistently has helped me embrace my inner detail-nerd, leveraging these assets in my client work as well as teaching and speaking to groups.

I was hungry to "figure me out." I continued learning all I could about Human Design because it was so brilliant at helping me understand myself, my unusual career, and my relationships. It gave me answers that made sense, plus a strategy for moving forward in my life that felt right to me. The more I learned, the more I was blown away. I quickly realized that there was nothing I wanted to do more in this world than help people through Human Design—to give them the sense of relief, peace, direction and confidence that I had found (things that Human Design uniquely provides).

For the first time in my life (at the beautiful age of 54) while studying Human Design, I finally had no doubt about what I wanted to do. A late bloomer, I guess, but that's okay. It was worth the wait! Since then, I have had the great honor of working with hundreds of people struggling to find their own answers—especially those facing big decisions or tough issues in their lives. Through our work they gain clarity, peace, relief, self-confidence, and a reliable way to find their own answers... answers specifically correct for THEM.

It's been both thrilling and humbling to share Human Design with so many heart-centered folks, ones who feel called to a mission or purpose though need help to clarify their specific direction. Often, what they get from their Reading is confirmation that they were already on the right track. It's priceless to finally relax into the direction that your soul has been nudging you. Human Design allows you to move forward with confidence and effectiveness in order to fulfill the contribution to the world that you were uniquely designed to make.

Human Design fully embodies the "teach a person to fish" parable. A Reading may not give you specific answers or solutions for immediate problems (which would "feed" you just for a day), but it teaches you HOW to make decisions and choose actions that align you with the truth and magnificence of who you are (so you know how to "feed" yourself for a lifetime). It's a huge difference.

Human Design is like a puzzle. It is a complex system of lots of little pieces that need to be understood individually, so then they can be put together into a coherent and meaningful whole picture about someone's life. I love figuring out and solving puzzles, particularly Sudoku puzzles because they require applying pure logic to determine the right answers. (I have Logic in my Chart and it likes to be used.) But my real love is crossword puzzles. There is something exquisite about that flash of insight when I figure out a clue and know I've found the right answer. The Sunday newspaper puzzles offer dozens of such exhilarating moments and I'm positively addicted. Being a Human Design practitioner and teacher allows me to use my beloved puzzle-solving skills to serve my fellow human beings in an exceptionally meaningful way. Life is good.

Within a few months of being introduced to Human Design in 2008, I enrolled in an intensive training course to study the system and learn how to give accurate, insightful, and empowering Human Design readings. To my surprise and great joy, I discovered how much studying Human Design, teaching it, and working one-on-one with clients really suit me. I dove enthusiastically into the deep details of Human Design and began doing Readings as soon as I could, supplementing my training with hands-on experience.

I was quickly certified at the highest level of that program and continue to expand my knowledge and skills by doing Readings, teaching courses, leading programs, and studying a variety of advanced Human Design course work. Despite having initial resistance to my personal Human Design *(I don't want to be a Projector... it's not fair... how am I supposed to build a successful business helping other people when I'm "just" a Projector?),* I've come to accept and finally LOVE my Chart and my design.

By the way, resisting one's Chart is a fairly common reaction. Many people think they would rather be a Type other than the Type they are. For example, some wish they were a Manifestor Type, making things happen in the world. But each Type has its own challenges as well as benefits. Relaxing into being exactly Who We Are is the most profound gift we can give ourselves and the world.

It's easy to talk about the power of Human Design knowledge, particularly Type and decision-making Strategy, but we really see the impact when applied directly in someone's life. Two of my clients (Catherine and Stephen) used their Type and Strategy information to improve their energy levels, their marriage of 27 years, and the art gallery they own and run together.

When Catherine came to me for a personal Reading, she was struggling. She was managing the gallery and her husband was the resident artist. She felt worn out from the routine operations of being there every day and she wasn't using her true brilliance for strategically increasing their business. They were even irritated with each other from things not running smoothly in their business.

Catherine, who is a Manifestor, is designed to initiate things and get the ball rolling, but not to do all the work of implementing and following through. As she learned her Type and Strategy, she realized it was not energetically correct for her to work "in" the gallery. She was much more effective (and happier) when she worked "on" the gallery with her innovative ideas and ability to make things happen. Although she had plenty of drive, her energy wasn't sustainable for tending to the daily operations of the business.

She began delegating more responsibility to their employee and spending less time in the gallery. Her husband, the artist, started spending more time there, which felt good to him and customers loved being able to talk with the artist himself.

In the past, their pattern for implementing new ideas to grow the gallery's business had been that Catherine would enthusiastically share a new idea with Stephen, maybe a new painting style, new subject matter, or different arrangement of the gallery, then he would begin the process of shifting his work or moving things around to implement her idea. But within no time, she would have several new ideas and be eager to implement those instead. As a Manifestor, that approach of "throwing spaghetti against the wall to see what sticks" is correct for her. She's designed to have lots of ideas and "try them on" but not necessarily fully implement or finish them.

Stephen is a Projector. He was exhausted from trying to keep up with her ideas and had "energetic whiplash" from the speed of her frequent changes in direction! It was a source of friction and frustration for them both. During his personal Reading with me, we worked on how he could manage his energy better now that he understood how much he is affected by the energy of others.

In their Relationship Reading, we analyzed both of their Human Design charts together (called a Composite Chart) and identified ways they could work together more effectively. They began to understand the dynamics of their two very different Types and Strategies and how to leverage this knowledge. They realized that Stephen should simply wait until some of Catherine's's ideas "stuck to the wall" before he began implementing, while Catherine agreed to "invite" him to implement something only when she felt clear and confident about pursuing that particular idea.

With this approach, their respective Types and Strategies were honored, their energies used correctly, and their friction and frustration dramatically reduced. They were so excited and grateful for this simple and sensible solution. Above all, the solution felt inherently right to both of them. Karen also told me that implementing her core Manifestor strategy of "inform before you act" had literally changed her life when she began applying it in all areas of her life.

Although we covered many details from their Charts during their Personal and Relationship Readings, simply knowing and applying their basic Type and Strategy information had the greatest immediate impact for them. This is one of the many reasons I love Human Design—it can be so simple in its application and power. Here are some of the other things I love about it:

- You learn it's possible to be the highest, fullest expression of every energy you carry in your Chart, and you finally have the tools to do exactly that.
- You see the beautiful synergy and synchronicity of each of us living our full potential and fulfilling our unique role.
- You see how YOU and each of us contribute magnificently (and vitally) to the well-being and evolution of the whole of humanity.

When we learn to live our lives according to our personal Type, Strategy, and Authority, we automatically align our decisions and actions with our fundamental energy structure. This allows synchronicity and flow in all areas of our lives. You find yourself in the "right" place at the "right" time, doing the "right" things as you discover and follow your path, play your role, and fulfill your uniquely configured purpose.

When everyone is living to their fullest potential as THEMSELVES, rather than struggling to be who they are not, we will live in a very different world. That is the world where I want to live. That is why I do this work of sharing, using and teaching Human Design. It profoundly helps humanity by helping us with our individual direction and clarity in life. You CAN know Who You Really Are and Why You Are Here. You CAN feel good in your skin and rejoice in being on YOUR correct path, whatever that is for you.

Even without knowing our Human Design, which most people don't, we often unconsciously express our Designs throughout our lives. But there is a catch. My story is a good example. My depth and details came naturally to me and paid off throughout my education and careers, but I was often living their "low expressions." For depth, my low expression was the fear of not knowing enough and not feeling ready. It was a paralyzing fear I wrestled many times. I have made real progress toward its higher expression by taming that fear and moving through it when it tries to get in my way. My low expression for details was (ironically) being so focused on details that I missed the big picture. I couldn't see "the forest for the trees," something I've been guilty of doing many times. I now work deliberately on its higher expression of maintaining a balance between these two perspectives.

Clearly, our personal Design is innate and very compelling, but knowing ourselves specifically through the foundational knowledge base of Human Design, makes life so much easier. Each energy defined (colored) in a Chart has a not only high vibration expression but also a low one in addition to a full range along the spectrum. Through this understanding, we see the clear choices we have.

All of my experiences and struggles, my high and low expressions, have shaped me into who I am today. It has all been a blessed journey of growth and awakening. I would not trade any part of what has happened to me. It took me a long time to be clear about my soul's mission in life, which is to empower people to know and love themselves. Helping others discover their Life Purpose and how to unfold it in ways that align with their natural energy is deeply fulfilling for them (and me). Through this work, I have learned that we are not broken; there is nothing to fix. We are perfect exactly as we are and powerful beyond measure. These truths are easy to see through the gift of Human Design, yet often hard to recognize without this profound self-knowledge.

You deserve to live the life of your dreams, and I truly want everyone to have this opportunity. I hope you will join us in transforming the world by transforming our own lives first. Self-knowledge and self-empowerment are the starting points on this journey of self-discovery. Our rewards for pursuing this journey include self-confidence, clarity, success, vitality, fulfillment, contribution, a sense of purpose, and great relationships.

Human Design is the most profound tool on the planet for helping us with this. Self-discovery and self-empowerment are personal journeys that have far-reaching (yes, global) impact and importance. I invite you to step up... and step into YOUR brilliant magnificence.

Welcome home.

Figure 15. Evelyn Levenson

Evelyn Levenson, M.B.A., M.P.A., is an emerging expert in the "new astrology" field of Human Design, an exciting new tool for personality assessment and life purpose discovery. She is a sought-after teacher, author and private consultant known for her warm and empowering style, actively sharing Human Design since 2008.

Evelyn is the creator of the "Success by Human Design" series of training courses that provide self-awareness and empowerment using this proven system of personal transformation. She is the author of *Human Design 101: A Crash Course in Aligning with Your Authentic Self,* a concise and practical tool for profound self-knowledge.

Combining 30+ years of business experience with a passion for uplifting and enriching people's lives, she delights in helping clients and students find and embrace the truth of Who They Are and Why They Are Here so they can fulfill their purpose and enjoy their lives with ease, grace, passion and success!

# Section 4
# Learning Abundance by Design

# Karen Curry Parker

# Understanding Your Human Design

Before you can begin to leverage your creative power, you have to first know who you are, how you operate, what you're here to do and how your energy is influenced by others. Your Human Design chart gives you this information and more.

## The Parts of the Human Design Chart

### Understanding the Chart

The Human Design chart, called the Body Graph, is a visual representation of the sum total of human possibilities and energies. The entire archetype of humanity is contained within the structural framework of the chart. All of the possibilities for the expression of being human appear here. The Body Graph shows us the different ways we love, hate, lead, follow, learn, know, grow and so much more!

Not only that, the chart shows your best strategy for making money, having great relationships, being healthy and staying creatively fulfilled. Your unique chart helps you understand how you work and how to best make your life work for you.

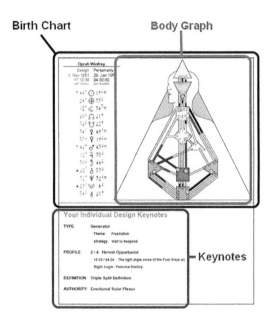

Figure 16. Human Design Chart

Each individual chart (calculated using your birth date, time and place) is a "map" of how you process energy. The chart reveals your strengths, your potential weaknesses, your gifts as well as talents. Most importantly, the chart tells the story of who you are, why you are here and how you can live a life that is true to who you really are. As we mentioned in Chapter One, everyone can get a free chart. Please visit GracePoint Matrix to get yours.

The story of each chart is based on the synthesis of everything in the chart. Each one is different and unique. It's in the sum total of all the parts of the chart that your personal energy "map" is revealed. Because of this, I highly recommend that you give yourself the gift of getting a full Human Design reading by a Human Design Specialist. Please find a Human Design Specialist here at GracePoint Matrix.

Human Design is rich and complex; it involves a lot of data. The system is a synthesis of Eastern and Western Astrology, the Chinese I'Ching, the Kabbalah, the Hindu Chakra System and Quantum Physics.

If you look at the chart closely, you might find visual evidence of some of the "parts" of Human Design. For example, if you turn the chart upside down it looks very similar to the Tree of Life from the Judaic Kabbalah.

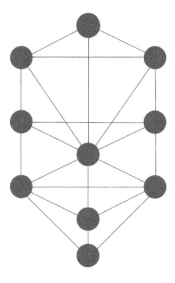

Figure 17. Kabbalah Tree of Life

Or you may notice that there are 64 numbers that appear on the Body Chart. These numbers, called Gates, correlate to the 64 Hexagrams from the Chinese I'Ching.

# Hexagram

Figure 18. I'Ching Hexagram

And, there are nine geometric shapes ("Centers") that appear on different parts of the body, similar to the seven energy centers of the Hindu Chakra system.

Figure 19. Hindu Chakra System

Even though you can see pieces of these ancient teachings in the chart, Human Design in and of itself is something new and unique. It's a brand-new tool to help people in a brand-new way.

Pulling all of the information together in synthesis is key to understanding Human Design as well as each individual chart. At its root, Human Design is a tool that teaches us about the power and possibility of evolution in mankind. There are learnings on a personal, relationship and collective level. The real beauty of Human Design is truly in the unification of all of its unique esoteric components.

The actual chart is also a synthesis of several parts that play together to give an overview of each individual. In order to "see" the big picture of a chart and to make learning about Human Design easier, we have to start first with taking the chart apart, piece by piece. Let's break down the parts of the chart into their individual components so you can begin to understand how the different pieces fit together.

Some of the individual pieces of the chart have energies that are similar but different on a subtle level. Please understand that as you learn about each part, we are (to a certain degree) taking pieces of the chart out of context. Each piece is important, but the full expression of each part will depend on what else is in your unique chart.

## The Nine Energy Centers

The first thing you will notice when you look at your chart is that there are nine geometric shapes. These shapes are called the nine Centers. Each Center carries and manages a certain frequency of energy and relates to specific themes in our lives. (We will discuss the function of each of these Centers in later chapters.)

## 9 Centers

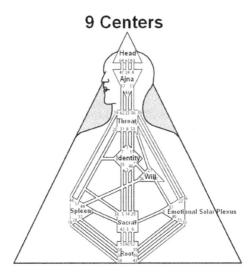

Figure 20. Nine Centers

If a Center is colored, then it is called defined. A defined Center has a consistent way of operating and is part of who you are. This is the energy that you radiate out into the world. It operates the same way energetically and thematically.

If a Center is white, then it is called undefined or "open." Open Centers are where we take energy and information in from the world around us. Not only do we absorb energies in our open Centers, we amplify them. In our open Centers, we experience others. It is in these open Centers that we have the potential for great wisdom but, as we will discuss in great depth in the chapter on Centers, also the potential for pain and confusion.

Your defined Centers represent aspects of your personality that are consistent and true about your personality all the time. It can be raining, Mercury can be in retrograde, Mars can disappear out of the solar system, but your definition always stays the same. These undefined areas represent aspects of your personality that are inconsistent. Where you are undefined is where you take in and amplify energy and information from other people.

For example, if you have an undefined emotional Solar Plexus (the triangle on the lower right-hand side of the Body Graph), you absorb other people's emotions and you feel them stronger than the person actually generating the feelings. Emotionally undefined individuals are empathic. With awareness, this empathy can be a great source of wisdom. Actually, any Center where you are undefined is potentially a great source of wisdom.

To illustrate my point, let me give you an example. I have an undefined emotional Solar Plexus. I hate going to movies because I bawl my eyes out every time. When I watched the movie, "Spirit, Stallion of the Cimarron" (an animated movie about a horse), I cried so hard during the whole movie that my nine-year-old daughter got up and moved to another seat because she was so disgusted by my emotional response. Honestly, it wasn't THAT sad a movie. What I now understand is that my open emotional system was taking in all the emotional energy in the theater and amplifying it. I was crying the tears for people in the whole theater.

While not helpful at a movie, it is critical in my life. In my coaching practice, this aspect of being emotionally undefined is a great asset for me. When I am assessing my client's emotional status, I KNOW what they are feeling because I am feeling it, too!

In another example when I worked as a nurse, this was very exhausting for me because I didn't understand my Human Design. I burned out very quickly because the emotional intensity was overwhelming and I would soak it up like a sponge. Now I use my emotional Solar Plexus as a screen, allowing all of that emotional information to pass through me. I don't hold on to it (meaning claiming it as my own) and I don't burn out.

Children who are emotionally undefined sometimes get labeled as being "dramatic." What they are doing is taking in all the emotional energy from the people around them and acting it out. I often see emotionally undefined children labeled as "disturbed" when they are, in fact, acting out the emotional health of their family or even emotional drama in their parent's marriage.

The beauty in the defined and undefined Centers lies in the fact that individually we are all simply puzzle pieces — parts of a greater whole. We all become completely defined when we are all together. We each bring pieces that energetically unify us all and offer us the opportunity to express all of the human experience.

You sense this when you go to a restaurant or a coffee shop. The designs of the customers and the staff blend together to make a collective aura.

Your definition comes from the position of the Gates and the planets at the moment of your birth. We can look at how the Body Chart and Centers integrate with your Conscious and Unconscious Birthday in the next section.

**The Numbers and Planets on the Chart**

On the left-hand side of the chart or flanking either side of the Body Graph (depending on which software you used to receive your free Human Design chart), you will see a series of red and black numbers along with planetary symbols.

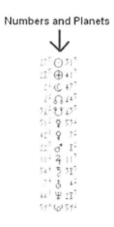

Figure 21. Numbers and Planets

You might also see that there are two birthdates located on your chart. The birth date in black is your actual birthday, called your Conscious Birthday in Human Design. (On some charts, the birthday may be in European format, i.e. day/month/year.) The **RED** birthday is called your Unconscious Birthday.

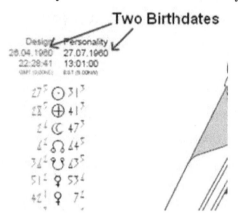

Figure 22. Two Birthdates

The numbers in **BLACK** are calculated on your actual birthday. This is your Conscious Design. The elements on the chart that are black are aspects of your personality of which you are consciously aware and, to a certain degree, over which you have some control.

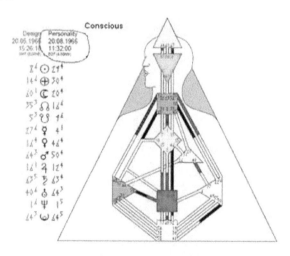

Figure 23. Conscious Design

The Unconscious Birthday (the one in **RED**) is calculated approximately 88 astrological degrees from the moment of your birth (roughly three months prior to your birth). This is the design of your Unconscious Personality.

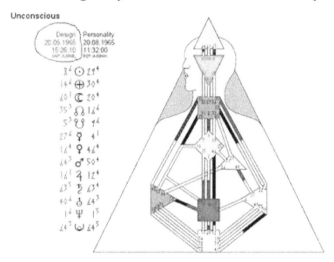

Figure 24. Unconscious Design

Your Unconscious Personality is defined by the red elements on the chart and represents aspects of your personality that are consistently part of who you are but are unconscious. This means you don't really have much control over these parts of your personality. Usually, with age, we become more aware of our Unconscious Personality. Your family and loved ones also usually know the Unconscious elements of who you are much sooner than you do yourself.

The planetary symbols indicate the astrological position of the energies in your chart at the moment of your birth. Your birth chart - the numbers alongside your Body

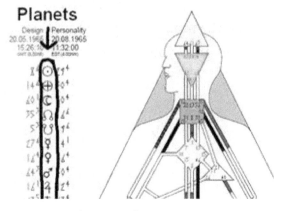

Figure 25. Planets

Graph - is fixed and does not change during the course of your whole life.

## The Channels

The next thing that you may notice on your chart is that it is covered with lines, some of them colored red, some black, some checkered black/red and some totally white.

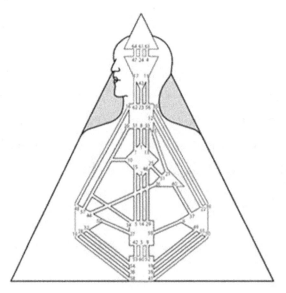

Figure 26. BodyGraph

Lines that span all the way between two Centers are called Channels. If you have a line that is colored to both ends (either solid black, solid red or checkered), then the Centers on either end of the channel will be defined (noted as being colored, too). An open (white) center has no fully colored channels attached to it.

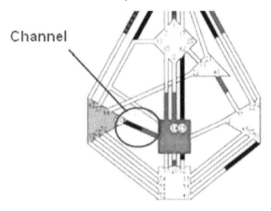

Figure 27. Channels

At the end of each line at the gateway for each channel, there is a Gate. There are 36 Channels in the Human Design body graph. Each channel has two halves called gates. There are a total of 64 Gates.

The 64 Gates correlate to the 64 Hexagrams in the Chinese I'Ching. Each active gate in your chart adds a different "flavor" to your personality.

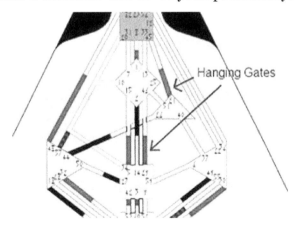

Figure 28. Hanging Gate

When only one gate in a channel is defined, it is called a Hanging Gate:

A Hanging Gate is always attracted to people who have the other half of the channel. This is called electromagnetic attraction.

You may notice that some of your Gates are colored differently. The black Gates are derived from the black numbers on the left of your Body Graph. Gates colored Black carry personality traits of which you are consciously aware. So for example, if you have the Gate 11 coming out of the Ajna Center towards the Throat colored black, then you would be consciously aware that you have a lot of ideas!

Some of the Gates on your body graph may be colored red. The red Gates are derived from the red numbers on the left side of your body graph. Again for example, if you have the Gate 13, The Gate of the Witness, as unconscious (red), then you may not be aware that your energy field communicates to others that they are safe to share their secrets with you. You probably have no idea why people are always coming up to you, out of the blue, and telling you their deepest, darkest secrets.

If you have checkered Gates, meaning the line to the Gate is in red and black, you express those particular personality aspects both in your conscious and unconscious definition whereas a white line represents an "open" Gate. You will always take in the energy of that open Gate from the world around you, and its expression through you will be inconsistent depending on your environment.

When you look at the numbers on the left side of the Body Graph, you will see that each Gate's number has a smaller number next to it. For each Gate, there are six different "lines" that are a further expression of your uniqueness. The lines of the Gates do not show up on the Body Graph, but their meaning can be revealed to you during a Human Design analysis. (You can refer back to the traditional Chinese I'Ching to gain more insight into each Gate.)

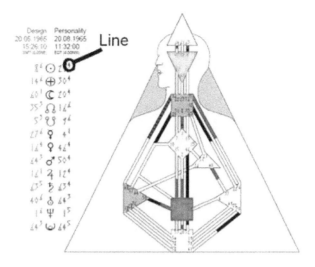

Figure 29. Line

## The Five Types

### Type

When you look at the bottom of your chart, you will see your type listed. There are five Types in the Human Design system. Each type has a specific Strategy for making powerful decisions.

The easiest way to begin benefiting from Human Design concepts is to know your Type. In the Human Design System, there are five personality "Types." Each has a unique Strategy for making decisions. Knowing your Type can help you develop confidence and trust in your capacity to make reliable decisions for yourself.

The five Types are: the Manifestor, the Manifesting Generator, the Generator, the Projector and the Reflector. Each Type has a different role to play when interacting with others and the world.

### The Manifestor

Approximately eight percent of all people are Manifestors and they can initiate action without waiting. Manifestors are energy beings that possess tremendous initiating power but they have to use their power carefully or risk angering others.

Their *purpose* in life is to initiate action. If a Manifestor decides to start a business, for example, all they have to do is decide on the right timing and then just do it. All of the other Types have to wait before they can take action.

In spite of the fact that most of us think we would love to be Manifestors, being a Manifestor can have its own challenges. Many Manifestors have struggled to learn to use their power appropriately and may be conditioned to hide their power (or suppress it entirely).

Manifestors must learn how to channel their energy properly or they will face tremendous resistance in life. Properly channeled, Manifestor energy often gives the other four Types ideas or projects needing response. Some famous Manifestors include Al Gore, George W. Bush, Jack Nicholson, Susan Sarandon and Johnny Depp.

## The Generator and The Manifesting Generator

The next two Types called Manifesting Generators and Generators are separate but reviewed together; they comprise 67% of the population. These two Types are the only Types are defined in the special energy center called the Sacral Center. Their purpose in life is to achieve mastery through repetition and work. They are the metaphorical "builders" of the world.

For both the Manifesting Generator and the Generator, the most important thing in life is finding the right work. If a Manifesting Generator or a Generator is not working in the right job, he will burn out. When these Types find the correct work, their Sacral Center supplies them with a virtually inexhaustible source of energy.

Manifesting Generators and Generators both have to wait for something to "respond to" before taking action. They can't efficiently use the phrase that most of us are taught: "just do it."

If we are Manifesting Generators or Generators we can experience deep frustration if we try to initiate things. For both of these Types, waiting for something to happen so we can respond is crucial for ensuring success. If Manifesting

Generators or Generators "just do it" in life, it is difficult to avoid burn-out from committing to the wrong work.

For example, a Generator who is a workshop facilitator might desire to teach a particular class. If this woman decides to initiate this workshop without anything "to respond to" other than her own mental urgings, most likely she will find that the workshop turnout may be low. Instead, if this Generator woman waits until someone suggests that she teach a workshop, she can respond to that suggestion and the outcome of the workshop will probably be much different.

Of course, waiting can feel very challenging for these energy types. It does not feel natural for most people to wait and see what life brings. If you are a Manifesting Generator or a Generator, it is best if you experiment with waiting (even if it is for just a few days and see what happens)!

With these two Types, your energy field communicates to the world that you need some suggestion so you can respond to it. When the Manifesting Generator and the Generator wait, things always come to them in the right time and the right way.

Even though these two Types are similar in how they must wait to respond in order to make decisions, there are some interesting differences between them. Manifesting Generators have some of the energy characteristics of Manifestors. They tend to respond more quickly to situations than a pure Generator.

Manifesting Generators may also have to "test drive" their response to situations that come to them in order to see if they are correct. Because of this characteristic of trying out responses, Manifesting Generators can seem as though they are changing their minds frequently.

Pure Generators act more deliberately when they respond, and they usually know what is correct for them to do without having to try it out first.

Some famous Manifesting Generators and Generators include Madonna, John Lennon, the Dalai Lama, Hillary Clinton, Oprah Winfrey and Timothy Leary.

## The Projector

Projectors represent about 24% of the population, usually becoming the natural managers and leaders of the world. Projectors do not carry energy in their own personal energy field but absorb the energies of others and manage it. Projectors have to wait to be recognized and invited into the major events in life, such as love relationships, career and right place (where they live).

If an invitation feels good for a Projector and she accepts it, she has her purpose: she channels an enormous amount of energy and power into that situation. She can then use that energy to manage others and the world around her.

Projectors are here to deeply understand others. Projectors can be powerful resources if they are recognized and used properly. A Projector can, simply by watching an energy Type, intuitively know how that other person can maximize their energy and their potential. This makes them natural coaches and mentors. Projectors are here to be recognized and invited by others. Many Projectors are magnetic, charismatic recipients of amazing invitations.

Though they have all this wisdom, Projectors can have a frustrating and debilitating life processes if they try to push themselves and initiate action. A Projector simply does not have the energy to "just do it" and if they try to initiate like a Manifestor (or work steadily like a Generator), they will burn themselves out very quickly.

The challenge for the Projector is to trust that the right invitations will come to them and to wait for those invitations. Sometimes Projectors wait months or years for the right invitation.

Because they are "non-energy" types and they are not here to work steadily like the Generator Types, Projectors may receive a lot of judgment from others and be perceived as "lazy" when, in fact, it is literally unhealthy for these types to initiate any kind of action or to work at the wrong kind of jobs on a steady basis. They usually can't sustain the energy flow on their own.

Ringo Starr is a Projector. He was literally "invited" to join The Beatles after one of the original band members left the band. Other famous Projectors include

Steven Spielberg, John F. Kennedy, Princess Diana, Fidel Castro, Karl Marx and Demi Moore.

### The Reflector

Less than one percent of people are Reflectors, making them the rarest of all five Types. The Reflector is here to "mirror" or reflect the health of the community around them. A Reflector is extremely open to all kinds of energy. The Reflector takes all the energy from the world around him deep into his own energy system and then reflects it back into the community.

If you are a Reflector and you are happy, then where you are at the moment is a happy place. If you are a sad Reflector then the community or the world around you is sad.

Because Reflectors are completely open, they can become very deeply wise about others and the world around them. Reflectors digest so much energy and information that it can take them a while to make decisions.

A Reflector needs to wait 28 days, the full cycle of a moon, before they can feel certain about their decisions. Sometimes, they have to wait out two or more moon cycles until they know a decision is correct for them.

Reflectors also need to talk about their decisions to everyone. Because they are always taking in information and processing it, it can be difficult for the Reflector to know herself. Reflectors have to see their decisions reflected through others in order to know what to do.

Famous Reflectors include Michael Jackson, Uri Geller and Roslyn Carter.

## The Additional Components of the Body Chart

### Strategy

Your Strategy comes from your Type. Strategy is the most important knowledge offered by your Human Design Chart. Your strategy is basically your personal way to make effective decisions. It gives you key information about how to operate your human vehicle in the world, how to make the right choices for you and how to recognize when you are on the right path in life.

Following your Strategy offers you the opportunity to experience events and circumstances that are correct for you. Not following the Strategy for your Type brings events and experiences into your life that may not be correct for you.

Because learning to follow strategy effectively can take months or years of practice, you can benefit from coaching by a Human Design Specialist who can provide you with feedback and encouragement.

Follow your Strategy and you will truly fulfill your Personal Destiny.

## Authority

Authority refers to an aspect of your design that influences your decision-making strategy. Although decision-making is tied directly to your Strategy, your Authority flavors the way you use your Strategy.

Authority is determined by certain Centers in your personal Body Graph that will have the most powerful influence on you when you make decisions. Not all Centers carry authority, so your personal authority will depend on your Type and your Definition.

Authority will also depend on your life conditioning and your level of emotional well-being. When you receive a Human Design Reading, you are taught to understand patterns of pain and behaviors that may be keeping you from living out the beauty of who you really are.

With cognitive awareness of old patterns, you begin to heal and transform these energies into deep sources of wisdom. The more you clear your old energy patterns the more effectively your natural decision-making skills (your Authority) can function. You can then begin to use your Authority along with your Strategy to help you make better decisions for your life.

## Profile

There are twelve different personality "Profiles" in the Human Design system. We derive an individual's Profile from the lines of the Gates in his or her conscious and unconscious Sun sign.

**Profile**

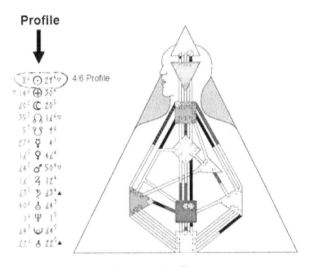

Figure 30. Profile

The Sun sign is the first sign on a chart under the "Design" and "Personality" columns. The lines are the little numbers just to the right of the big numbers. They look like exponents or a number being raised "to the power of" in mathematics. Profiles tell you about major life themes that you will encounter, and they illustrate another way in which your personality interacts with the world. Everyone comes into the world with a specific Profile and purpose. Knowing your Profile can help you see some of the themes that you will encounter as you move toward fulfilling your purpose.

Each number in a Profile has a specific meaning. The first number in your Profile is an element of your personality of which you are you will be consciously aware. This number comes from the black numbers on your chart, called the "Personality." The second number in the Profile may be unconscious and more hidden from you. The second number is derived from the red numbers on your chart called the "Design."

The twelve Profiles are derived from the six possible lines of a particular Gate. Each of these six lines represents a different archetype or style of behavior. Your Profile can be thought of as an explanation of your conscious and unconscious archetype and the themes associated with that archetype. Most people are aware of their unconscious Profile but because it is unconscious, they do not have a lot of real control over the expression of it.

## Definitions of the Lines

Here are basic definitions for each of the six Profile Lines:

**Line 1 - Investigator**
**Line 2 - Hermit**
**Line 3 - Martyr**

**Line 4 - Opportunist**
**Line 5 - Heretic**
**Line 6 - Role Model**

The twelve Profiles listed below are combinations of two of those lines (the "conscious" line followed by the "unconscious" line).

**1/3 Investigator/Martyr**
**1/4 Investigator/Opportunist**
**2/4 Hermit/Opportunist**
**2/5 Hermit/Heretic**
**3/5 Martyr/Heretic**
**3/6 Martyr/Role Model**

**4/6 Opportunist/Role Model**
**4/1 Opportunist/Investigator**
**5/1 Heretic/Investigator**
**5/2 Heretic/Hermit**
**6/2 Role Model/Hermit**
**6/3 Role Model/Martyr**

## Emotional Theme

Each Human Design Type has an emotional theme. The emotional theme is simply part of a person's life and brings them lessons and opportunities for growth. When you experience your emotional theme in a strong way, it's usually a sign that you are not living true to yourself. It's always good to take a step back and evaluate your life if you're feeling your emotional theme in a powerful way.

When you live your life according to your Human Design Strategy, you lessen the intensity of your experience of your emotional theme. You might feel it here and there but it won't be a roaring monster that dogs you day and night. Following your Strategy makes your entire life experience easier and more enjoyable.

The emotional theme is thematic. That means that you will either be experiencing the emotions of your theme yourself, or you may be experiencing them in other people around you who are responding to your behavior.

So, for example, if you are a Manifestor Type, the Manifestor has an emotional theme of anger. A Manifestor has a Strategy of needing to inform people before they do things (a hard thing for a Manifestor). It can make a Manifestor feel a little angry that they have to inform someone before they "do" but they will experience a lot less anger directed AT them if they inform first.

We will discuss the emotional themes when we talk more about Type.

## Incarnation Cross

The final piece of the Chart that ties the whole thing together is called the Incarnation Cross, which is comprised of the energies that make up the Conscious and Unconscious Sun and Earth (which is found in the second row in those columns beside in the chart).

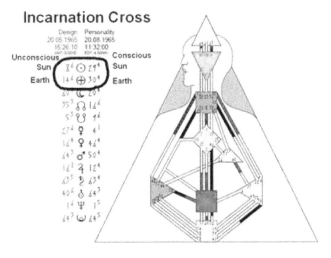

Figure 31. Incarnation Cross

These four energies combined comprise about 70% of the personality expression of a person. The Incarnation Cross in a chart is basically the archetype of a person. It tells us who they are, what they are driven to do, their foibles, follies and ultimately their destiny, if they choose.

The top four numbers on your Human Design chart are called your Incarnation Cross. There are 768 different variations of Incarnation Crosses. Your Incarnation Cross tells you very specific things about your unique life purpose and your destiny. Because each Incarnation Cross is unique and also integrates with the elements in your specific chart, really getting to the heart of your Incarnation Cross is something you can only do with an experienced Human Design Specialist. Your Human Design Specialist can look at your chart with your Incarnation Cross and weave together a story to help you understand who you are, what you're here to do and what you need to do to step into the full mastery of your destiny.

## Definition

Energy in a Chart can be connected and unified or split into separate groupings. Energy Centers that are connected by colored channels belong to a defined grouping. If there is at least one colored channel connecting two energy centers, and those centers are also connected by a colored channel to a different energy center - that is one definition. In many charts, there are separate groupings that are connected within themselves but not connected to each other. This creates a "split" in the definition of the chart.

When all of your defined Gates and Channels are connected to each other you have a "single definition" energy configuration.

When you have "single definition" it means that you sense of yourself is more unified and singular and you don't feel like you have a lot of distinctly different aspects to your personality.

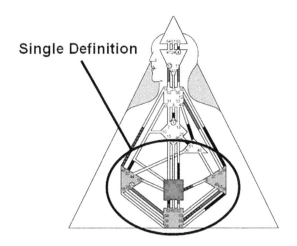

Figure 32. Single Definition

Charts can also have a "split definition" energy configuration. "Split definition" means that you have two (or more) "groupings' of Centers and Channels in your chart that are not connected to other "groupings' of energy in your chart. You can have up to four different groups of energy splits in a chart.

When you have a "split definition," it can feel like you have several distinctly different drives and aspects to your personality. Each "split" or energy grouping is magnetic and is attracted to people who bring the Gates that unify the "splits". When you get your splits connected, your energy feels more lined up and unified.

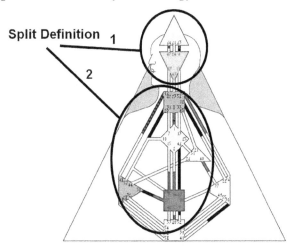

Figure 33. Split Definition

Triple Split Definition means that there are three distinct groupings of Energy Centers that are independent (not connected to each other). Here is an example of a Triple Split Definition.

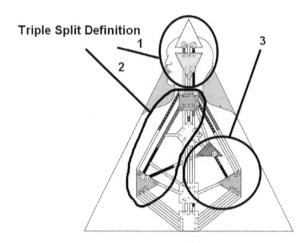

Figure 34. Triple Split Definition

Quadruple Split means that there are four distinct groupings of Energy Centers that are independent and not connected to each other. People with Quadruple Split definition are fairly rare, though this is an example of a Quadruple Split Definition.

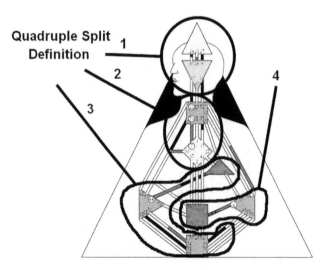

Figure 35. Quadruple Split Definition

An energy split can make you feel like you have certain very distinct different aspects to your perception of yourself. For example, in the Split Chart, you may feel like you have a very powerful mind and can get "lost in your head" while that you also have an "earthy" and kind of primal part of your personality as well.

In relationships, you are often attracted to partners who have the Gates that "bridge" your splits. When these Gates are defined in a partner, in that particular relationship you feel "whole" or like all the parts of yourself are unified (which is indeed what happens, at least energetically).

## Conclusion

The parts of the Chart are each, in and of themselves, important and give key insights into a personality. Understanding each part and the role it plays in the story in the story of your life, helps you put together a bigger picture and deeper understanding of who you truly are.

Remember, each part is a piece of a whole. While we have to "take the chart apart" in order to understand all of its key pieces, the real beauty in the chart is in the synthesis of all of the parts. The true story of who you are is revealed when all of the pieces come together.

The next sections of this book are designed to give you a practical guide to deepening your awareness of your True Self and specific exercises and strategies to begin embracing what is right about you and your life. My intention is to support you in connecting with your authentic self in a new and empowered way and helping you stay resilient during times of change.

You can download the worksheets and exercises shared in the following chapters by going here: gracepointmatrix.com/abundance-worksheets/.

# Karen Curry Parker

# The Human Blueprint for Abundance

There are two very important concepts in Human Design that help you understand who you are, how you process energy and ultimately what may be keeping you from allowing yourself to align with your natural state of abundance.

When you look at your Human Design chart, you will see that you have parts that are colored in and parts that are white. The colored in parts are aspects of your energy that you experience consistently. These are the energies that determine your Human Design energy Type and your Life Purpose.

The parts of your chart that are white, or "undefined," are the places in your energy blueprint where you absorb energy from the world around you. We are all designed to experience each other and to interconnect. The undefined places in our charts are how to experience and know each other and consequently, they have the potential to help us gain wisdom about the possibilities of the human experience.

Because we all have defined and undefined parts of the Body Graph, the chart can be viewed as a map or blueprint for what is possible for humanity. The chart tells us about what is natural and true for all humans.

If you view the chart from this perspective, what you see is that everyone is designed to be abundant and that being abundant is part of our natural state.

When you understand the way the Chart works and the promise that it holds for abundance for all of us, it helps you combat the doubt that you can experience when you face temporary challenges in abundance.

Before we can look at the mechanics of abundance in the chart, we have to start with some basic esoteric Human Design knowledge and some important general assumptions.

**Assumption #1:** We live in an infinitely abundant universe where the possibilities to express creative force are a part of our nature.

**Assumption #2:** The nature of the universe is to grow and evolve. We thrive when we are challenged.

**Assumption #3:** As individual expressions of the universe, we have within us an infinite capacity to create.

**Assumption #4:** Because being infinite in our creative capacity is pretty overwhelming for humans, we have unique Human Designs that "limit" our creative capacity so that what we create is within more finite guidelines. (Trust me, you LIKE being a little limited, and we are still capable of creating and growing a heck of a lot!!)

**Assumption #5:** Your unique Human Design plays a very important role in the big picture of the universe. There is no one like you. There has never been anyone like you. There will never be anyone like you again.

**Assumption #6:** You are designed to interface with the unfolding of the universe. Your Human Design anchors you in the infinite and helps you connect with your growth, evolution and your capacity to create.

Figure 36. Assumptions

In the Human Design chart, there are nine energy Centers. Each Center is responsible for processing different kinds of energy. The Centers correlate loosely to the Hindu Chakra system.

The diamond shaped Center in the middle of the chart is called the G-Center or the Identity Center. The G-Center is the center for love and direction in the chart. The G-Center has a magnetic energy that emanates from within it. This special magnet only attracts. It does not repel.

The purpose of the G-Center is to attract into your life all of the experiences, resources, connections and power you need to live abundantly. What the G-Center attracts into your life is determined by eight key energies that are anchored in the G-Center. These eight key energies attune the G-Center and influence what the G-Center calls into your life experience.

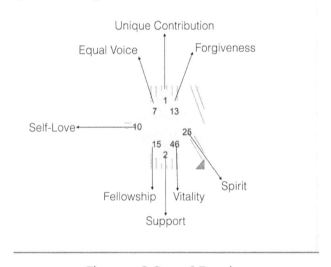

Figure 37. G-Center 8 Energies

These eight energies are derived from the eight Gates that surround the G-Center. Ultimately, what the G-Center attracts is determined by:

1. How much you love yourself (Gate 10 - The Gate of Self Love).
2. How powerful you feel. (Gate 7 - the Gate of Leadership Support).
3. How authentically you are expressing yourself in your life (Gate 1 - Creative Contribution).

4. How much you have released the pain of the past and found the blessings (Gate 13 - Forgiveness).

5. How much you trust Spirit as Source in your life (Gate 25 - the Love of Spirit).

6. How physically vital you feel and how grounded you are in your body (Gate 46 - Embodiment).

7. How much you believe that you deserve to receive all the resources you need to fulfill your destiny (Gate 2 - the Receptive).

8. How much your choices are not only good for you but benefit humanity (Gate 15 - The Love of Humanity).

In other words, in the highest expression of human potential, we are designed to be fully engaged with our lives. It happens with a zest that allows us to evolve by learning from and leaving the past behind, loving and valuing ourselves, by consciously and consistently expressing our authentic potential and making our unique contribution to the world. It allows us to take our direction from Spirit, to be physically vital, to allow (and receive) all the resources we need to fulfill our destiny and to take actions that are only for the greater good of the world.

If you are out of alignment in any of these eight areas, your G-Center will attract into your life opportunities to master these energies.

To get a deeper appreciation of how this energy Center influences your life experiences, we have to revisit Assumption #2 and how it works. *Assumption #2 states that "The nature of the universe is to grow and evolve. We thrive when we are challenged."*

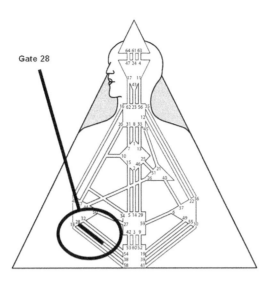

Figure 38. Gate 28

We are designed to be challenged as part of our growth cycles in life. We are not designed to suffer as part of our growth, but to struggle sometimes to discover what is truly meaningful in life. This energy for struggle, located on the Gate 28 in the chart, is also the energy for adventure, game-playing and the drive to do what you need to do because you understand what is worth the struggle or battle. We grow, evolve and transform as a result of struggle. If we aren't challenged, as uncomfortable as it can make us feel sometimes, we stagnate.

(Remember, we aren't looking at the Body Graph in the context of your unique chart just yet. We are still talking about the chart as a blueprint for the human experience.)

Let's go back to the G-Center and the alignment to abundance that happens with the eight key energies of the G-Center.

It's easiest when we use a concrete example. Let's say you are struggling with self-love (like most people on the planet). The level of self-love that you are feeling attunes the magnet in your G-Center. Your G-Center is now programmed to attract into your life opportunities for you to learn to love yourself.

As a result, you may find that you keep attracting all the "wrong" partners into your life — partners who don't love, value and respect you. That experience has two potential reactions from you. You can either, keep focusing on the fact that you aren't "good" at attracting the right people into your life and bemoan the fact that "no one loves you."

Or, you can see that these relationships are a reflection of your self-love and recognize that, before you date another person, maybe you need to clean up your own sense of your lovability so you can attract to yourself a different kind of experience and a better partner.

Many of you may have been working very keenly on living out the highest expression of the eight key energies of the G-Center. While you have probably made some progress, you are mostly trained to try to tackle these key areas with your thinking and your mindsets. Later on in this book, you'll learn why trying to mentally master these eight key energies is a largely ineffective way to grow and evolve.

The secret to aligning with your natural state of abundance and fulfilling the highest potential of the human experience is not as difficult or tricky as you may believe. The answer to living your unique abundance requires you to simply follow your Human Design Strategy according to your Type. Become aware of your unique energy configuration and how it influences what you desire in life, what you believe is possible and what kinds of actions you take to create the abundance you deserve.

If we are designed to be abundant, why is it then that so many of us struggle to access that as our natural state? There are several common "blocks" or patterns that keep us stuck. This limits our access to our natural abundance.

The most powerful thing that keeps us from creating what we want in our lives is being out of alignment with who we really are. We are designed to experience our unique, perfect state of abundance when we are living true to our life purpose and our Human Design.

You are perfectly hardwired to tap into the universal flow of abundance in the way that's right for you when you are fulfilling your potential, doing what you came here to do and doing it in the way that's correct for you.

If you are trying to be someone you are not, do something you don't want to do or you are out of alignment with your energy blueprint, you may struggle with creating what you want in life.

It takes an enormous amount of energy to try to be someone you're not. Anytime you say "yes" to things when you want to say "no" or anytime you say "no" to things knowing you want to say "yes," your energy field has to adjust to this misalignment. Think of it as being a kind of "inflammation" of the energy field.

The universal flow of abundance is inherently loving and nurturing. It's also pretty literal and linear. If you aren't doing what you want to do, it frequently results in you hating your life as well as being exhausted from making choices based on a series of motivations and drives that aren't congruent with your soul's purpose in this lifetime. The universe often manifests "stuck-ness" because it's giving you a chance to sit still and get clear about what you want.

Remember, sometimes we have to push and struggle to grow and get clarity.

But what often happens is we misinterpret the support that the universe is sending us and we get angry, frustrated, and bitter or disappointed that life doesn't seem to be unfolding the way we want it to happen. We don't realize that the reflection of our life circumstances is actually showing us clearly where we aren't aligned with our true selves or where we don't have faith that we can actually have what we really want in life.

When we are in perfect alignment with our true selves, our energy is aligned and the flow of abundance is easy and natural as it's designed to be. The desire to move forward and the faith that what we want will manifest feels easy. We don't struggle with procrastination, lack of energy, avoidance or any other emotions that keep us from doing what's necessary to make our dreams come true.

The second problem in manifesting our abundance is that before we are even born, we are deeply imprinted by outside energies and belief systems that make it confusing to connect with our authentic selves. In Human Design, we call this imprinting "Conditioning" and it is a mechanical process that can be explained and understood in a precise way, taking out the guesswork in understanding who you are and what influences you away from your authentic expression.

There are five kinds of Conditioning in Human Design.

1. Open-ness by Centers
2. Imprinting
3. Generational Energy Patterns
4. Genetics
5. Design Crystal

## Open-ness by Center

The most common and predictable kind of Conditioning comes from what we call "open-ness" in the chart. We all experience this kind of Conditioning. The trick is being aware of it and learning how to use it to become wise about the energies surrounding you.

When you look at your Human Design chart, you will see that you have some parts that are colored ("defined") and some parts that are white. Anything that is defined is energy to which you have consistent access and that you experience in a fixed, immutable way. Your definition in your chart is your authentic self.

Your definition is also the energy that you broadcast out into the world and the part of your energy that people feel and experience the most from you. All energies in the chart that are defined are sustainable; you are able to draw on those energies all of the time.

The parts of your chart that are white and lack color are called "undefined" or "open." The open-ness in your chart is where you experience energy in a fluid, mutable way. Where you have open-ness is where you draw energy and information from the world around you.

It's in your open-ness in your chart that you experience other people's energies and consequently, your open-ness is where you can be deeply wise about other people's energy.

You don't simply feel other people's energy in your open Centers. You actually amplify energy in your open Centers to the effect that you experience your "open" energy in an intense way that can often "override" your own definition in your chart and your connection with your authentic self.

Because we have such intense feelings in our open Centers, we often get confused about the "owner" of the energy in our open Centers. In our open Centers, we merge with other people's energies, causing our own energy and beliefs systems to possibly get "hijacked" by outside influences.

Open Centers have very predictable conditioned behavioral patterns (discussed more in the next chapter). When you understand your open Centers, you can stop allowing your energy to get overrun by someone else's. You can start living out the wisdom of your open-ness instead of the pain.

## Imprinting

Imprinting happens on multiple levels of your being. We are imprinted in utero by the energy and circumstances of our mother and our genetic lineage. The emerging science of epigenetics has revealed that our DNA is actually influenced by the life experiences of our ancestors and, in particular, our maternal grandmothers.

We are also energetically imprinted by the people we grow up with. The Human Design of your parents will influence how you perceive your own energy. For instance, if your parents are a different Human Design Type than you, it's possible that you may mistakenly think that you are the same Type as your parents (consequently losing your connection with the purpose and energy of your own Type).

You will also pick up your parents' energies in your open Centers. Because you'll be influenced by their energy over the course of your childhood, it becomes very easy to feel like you have energies that you don't. When you leave home (which means also leaving your parent's aura), your own energy changes. You may find that you don't have access to energy that you experienced and with which you identified when you were younger. This change in energy can be very confusing, even disorienting; sometimes, it can cause you to push even harder with energy you don't have to try to be like your family, only to find that you really can't tap into that same energy anymore.

## Generational Energy Patterns

We inherit our Human Design from our grandparents. If you are able to see your grandparents' charts, you will notice certain energy themes from their charts that you have in your own chart. Your parents have also inherited their design from their grandparents (your great-grandparents).

This pattern sets us up perfectly to repeat intergenerational family dynamics over and over again. You will have the same energy patterns with your parents as you will have with your children. Your children will have the same patterns with you as they have with their children and so on.

What this means is that sometimes your behavioral patterns have come from generations of your family acting and reacting in specific ways, using familial belief systems and patterns handed down from parent to child for many years.

## Genetics

Your genetics (your physical DNA) will also influence your experience of abundance. The emerging science of epigenetics shows that our gene expression is often influenced by our life experiences, belief systems held by our families, our sense of connection within a community and by a meaningful connection with our authentic selves.

The more we heal our pain and trauma, the more things improve. When we align belief systems toward believing in the abundance of the universe as well as affirming the value of who we are, feel connected, believe we are loved by a tribe of people who value us and we live true to who we are, the healthier we become. This makes it less likely we are to experience the negative programming stored in our genes.

In the following chapters, you will discover practical and easy ways to live more true to who you really are and more fully tap into the abundant nature of Life. Let's start the process together with this exercise about the eight keys of the G-Center.

## Ranking Exercise:

Rank yourself on the eight keys of the G-Center. On a scale of 0-10, with 10 being the highest score, how would you rank yourself on the following energetic characteristics:

Self Love

Empowerment

Authenticity

Ability to let go
of the past

Connected to Spirit

Physically vital

Trusting and
allowing

Contributing to
humanity

Figure 39. Ranking Exercise

## Journaling Exercise

**How deeply do you trust the abundant nature of the universe?**

**What needs to be released/healed for you to relax and trust the abundant flow of your life?**

Figure 40. Journaling Exercise

# Karen Curry Parker

# The Five Human Design Types and Abundance

Imagine this: Close your eyes; in your mind's eye envision a bountiful, flowing river. That river is your abundance. To be in the flow of this "river of abundance," you have many options. You can jump in, swim across, float on an inner tube, scoop water into buckets to carry home, cross the river via bridge or stones placed in strategic places...There are many ways to enjoy the river.

The energy of abundance is just like this river. It's steady, ample, fluid and moving in an expansive way. There are an infinite number of ways to enjoy this river. But to really get the most out of this river, you have to discover the way that is easiest and works best for you.

Maybe you've rented a jet ski, but you hate the sound they make and the speed at which they travel so you realize you'd really rather be kayaking. You're not going to get the most out of the river. If you're trying to swim across but you don't have the strength and the endurance, being in the river might even kill you.

The problem isn't that the river is dangerous or only accessible to an exclusive group of people. The problem is that you're trying to get into the river in a way that you don't enjoy and isn't making the best use of your energy.

Abundance is like a song that is just waiting for a composer and musicians to come along to play it. It's steady, consistent and always accessible to us.

But you have to interface with your abundance in the way that's right for you.

For years we've been teaching people that your thoughts, works, actions and beliefs create your reality that you determine how you interact with the flow of abundance. While I agree 100% that this is true, that's only part of the story. There is more to aligning with the natural flow of abundance than just using our minds and creating out of our heads.

You have to also be aligned with your specific mechanical way of interfacing with the river of abundance. We all get into the flow of the river differently. For you to stay consistently and sustainably abundant, you have to be living true to your Human Design and your unique energy blueprint.

As you've seen there are many potential combinations in a Human Design chart:

5 Types

6 Authorities

9 Centers

12 Profiles

36 Channels and 64 Gates

768 variations of Incarnation Crosses

You are a unique combination of all of these elements. Understanding yourself and the intricate subtleties of your chart is a beautiful and worthwhile process. But, in the name of keeping it simple, the most important (and easy) element that you need to know to help you activate the full nature of your abundance is your Human Design Type Each of the five Types has a special way of creating and experiencing abundance. Your Human Design Type is the fundamental essence of your energy structure. Your Type determines how you manifest as well as what kind of things you need to do to stay aligned with your abundance, your purpose and your wealth theme.

Your Human Design Type carries a specific "vibration" that calls into your life the exact kinds of experiences you need to have to engage with your abundance in a way that is joyful and sustainable. But you have to act in ways that are true to your

Type in order to experience the full effect of your energetic "vibration."

When we don't act or live true to our Type, it can actually push support away and make it challenging to step into the river of abundance that is waiting for us. So many times we think when things don't work out that we are "broken" or blocked. In reality, what I've found over the years is simply that we aren't accessing our abundance correctly. Following your Strategy according to your Human Design Type is all that's necessary to "fix" what seems to not be working.

Your Type sets the stage for your abundance. It tells you how your energy works, what you need to do to tap into your abundance correctly, key strategies for sustaining abundance in your life (so that you can avoid "boom and bust" cycles or burnout) and your wealth theme. When you live true to your Type, you create flow, experience opportunities, receive unexpected blessing and take the right action.

With the five Types in the Human Design System, each Type has a different role, quality of energy, theme and unique challenges. Understanding your Type is the most important information you need to know about your Human Design. If you live true to your energy Type, all of the other pieces of your chart will come together.

The Types are classified in two distinctly different categories, the Open Sacral Types and the Sacral Types. The Open Sacral Types do not have sustainable work force and life force energy and, as such, are not designed to work in the traditional way that we define "work" and have a tendency to burn out when they try to create success in the traditional way we are taught to be successful.

The Sacral Types do have sustainable work force and life force energy but they are not designed to push and force things to happen. They have sustainable energy for working but have to wait until the right circumstance and opportunities show up. Because we are all trained to "manifest" our destinies, most Sacral Types have not waited for the right work and are often stuck and frustrated working jobs that they hate and confused about how to really create work that they love and that creates true abundance in their lives.

In the next section of this chapter, you will learn about each of the categories and the Types. You'll discover each Type's life purpose, wealth theme, strategy, emotional theme and challenges plus some simple strategies to help each Type get aligned with their natural wealth.

Each Type has a unique life purpose and decision-making strategy, crucial for making correct choices that are in alignment with your way of creating abundance.

Every Type also has an emotional theme. Your emotional theme is the most common emotion you experience, both from within yourself and from others. You will always experience this emotional theme, even if you live completely true to yourself. The key is to understand the nature of your emotional theme and to not let it create a self-destructive emotional reaction.

Your wealth theme is what each Type needs to honor and allow in order to create abundance. If you are not following your wealth theme, you're not accessing the full potential of your energy and your abundance in a way that is sustainable, healthy or joyful.

# The Open Sacral Types: The Manifestor, the Projector and the Reflector

## Manifestor Type

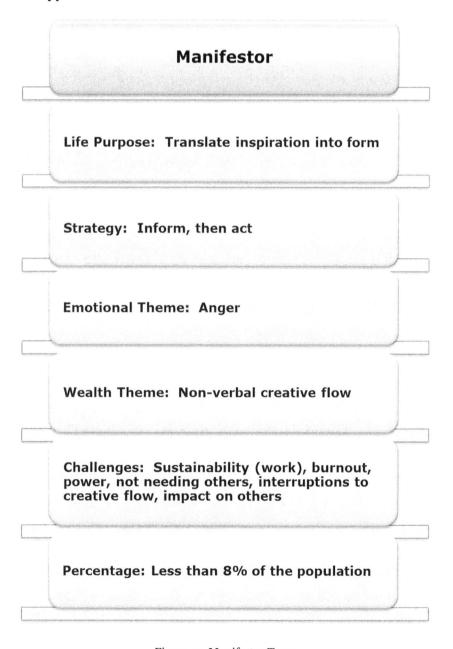

Figure 41. Manifestor Type

The life purpose of the Manifestor is to initiate action and creation. The Manifestor is uniquely different from all of the other Types in that the Manifestor is the only Type who doesn't have to wait for an outside force to help them recognize right timing.

Manifestors have an inner creative process, one that is non-verbal and difficult to explain. Since it's hard to express to others, answering questions or asking for help is difficult for a Manifestor because they have a hard time explaining what you're doing.

When a Manifestor is creating, they are simply moving. The timing of their movement is internal and is very attuned to their unique creative flow. Once a Manifestor gets an idea, in order to make it happen all they have to do is wait for the timing to feel right and then take action.

In addition, it is the role of the Manifestor to process inspiration and translate it into action. It is the role of the Manifestor to make an idea happen, even if they don't finish the job or do the grunt work associated with the manifestation of an idea (that's the role of the Generator Types), it's their job in life to get the proverbial ball rolling. When they don't, it can actually cause them to shut down their creative energy and their power to manifest abundance.

Because Manifestors are often following their own inner creative flow (and consequently, deeply attuned to their own process), it's easy for other people to misunderstand or misinterpret the Manifestor energy. This particular Type can make life easier for others (and their loved ones) if they learn to inform before they follow their creative impulses.

Informing isn't natural or easy. Manifestors often have their energy shut down or their creative impulse judged or squashed. Because of this, many Manifestors learn to hide their power and even hide what they're really doing. Manifestors are not here to be stopped or told what to do.

They may have also felt that taking the time to find the words to express their creative flow is so difficult that it's easier for them to do things for themselves than it is for them to try to find the words to ask for help. It can also be difficult if someone with the best of intentions tries to help them. In response to assistance, the Manifestor can feel angry if they have to stop what they're doing in order to try and find the words to describe it to someone else.

This can sometimes lead to other people thinking that Manifestors are self-absorbed or not "team players." Neither of these things is necessarily true. It's simply that the Manifestor is "in their own flow" and if they have to stop for some reason, they know that they might not pick it up again in the same way.

Manifestors are often afraid to tell people what they are doing, as often they have a lifetime experience of people trying to stop or control them. Especially as children, they learn to quietly do what their creative impulse tells them to do. But, when the Manifestor fails to inform, it makes the emotional theme of anger much more prevalent in their lives. People get confused by what the Manifestor is doing and then this Type reacts negatively. Manifestors need to inform and they also need to follow their creative flow, no matter what anyone else thinks or says. This can be hard for sensitive Manifestors.

To stay connected with their abundance, Manifestors have to take the action that feels right to them — no matter what anyone else thinks or says.

Manifestors do not have sustainable energy. They need cycles of rest and restoration. Consequently, working (in the traditional way we think of as working) isn't healthy or even profitable for the Manifestor; they do well with work that involves getting something started and then moving on or handling the type of work that is cyclical in nature. Because of this, burnout can also be a challenge for Manifestors.

## Projector Type

**Projector**

**Life Purpose:** Manage and guide creation

**Strategy:** Wait to be invited/recognized, act

**Emotional Theme:** Bitterness

**Wealth Theme:** Mid-wife to universe, facilitate

**Challenges:** Sustainability, patience, self-worth, trust abundance of universe, follow your bliss, not knowing self, needing recognition, burn out

**Percentage:** 20% of the population

Figure 42. Projector Type

Projectors can have the hardest challenge when it comes to abundance. Part of the reason for this challenge is that the Projectors have a unique role that is often misunderstood or misinterpreted and the Projector Strategy is one of the most counterintuitive of all the Human Design Types.

Projectors have a life purpose of managing and guiding others in their process of creation.

Projectors are inherently intuitive and wise about others. A Projector can watch any of the three energy Types (Manfiestor, Generator and Manifesting Generator) and instantly be conscious of what needs to happen to make their impact and work more effective and easier.

This is a natural and intricate part of the Projector personality. If you watch young children Projectors, they manage their parents and their peers with great awareness and clarity. This can often earn them the reputation of being "bossy," controlling or a "know it all."

The reason why this inherent wisdom is often misunderstood is because collectively we don't know how to make the most of the energy of the Projectors.

The Projector Strategy is to wait to be invited into the big opportunities in life. These big invitations come infrequently, every two to three years. Big opportunities are things like love, marriage, moving, getting a new job, etc. In between the big invitations, Projectors don't have to wait for small things such as going to a movie or going out to eat.

Unlike Generator Types that have to wait to respond to everything (including the small things in life for them to be in alignment with abundance) or Manifestor Types that have to wait for their creative flow to feel right, Projectors don't have to wait for anything except big invitations. Waiting for those big invitations is an important part of helping the Projector find the place in life where they are valued and loved for who they really are. Manifestors have to wait for their creative flow to feel right, but again, that's not how a Projector functions.

Projectors are not here to manage and guide everyone. They have their own group of people or "tribe" who is waiting for them to come manage them. To find their "people," Projectors have to be recognized or invited into sharing their wisdom.

In a society where we are taught to go out and make life happen, waiting for recognition and invitations from others can feel like a painful and agonizingly slow process. Because Projectors are often trained to act differently than their true nature, they can get very busy pushing and forcing people to see and recognize them. This often forces missing true invitations when they come because they're too busy doing what they've been trained that they "need" to or "should" by others.

But pushing and forcing never works for Projectors. In fact, pushing and forcing will always have the opposite effect for Projectors. The more a Projector pushes and forces and struggles to be seen and recognized, the more invisible they become.

Not only that, Projectors have a very finite amount of energy. They are not designed to work in the traditional way that we define work and can burn out easily. Especially if a Projector's work doesn't recognize their inherent, intuitive gifts or involves hard physical labor of any kind, they can burn out fast.

Projectors can't make life work for them if they follow the standard definitions of what it takes to be successful in life, although Projectors can be powerful and very successful. (For example, President Obama and President Kennedy are both Projectors.)

Because pushing and forcing for Projectors actually pushes people away rather than attracts people and because working hard isn't really an option for the limited energy of the Projector, no matter how hard they try, the Projector can often feel that life isn't "fair," which may cause them to become bitter.

In addition, because very few Projectors are taught how to properly access their energy, of all the Type groups, they can often be the most challenged when it comes to abundance.

There are two key factors in creating abundance for the Projector. First of all, the most important thing that a Projector has to master is their own sense of worth and value. A Projector has to wait to be recognized by the right people — the people who value and see them for the gifts they bear. If a Projector is not sitting and waiting for the right people because they question their own value, it makes them bitter and ultimately causes them to "waste" their wisdom and energy on people who don't value who they are.

Projectors who value themselves enough to wait for the right people to give them invitations are powerfully compelling and often have to turn invitations away. A Projector who values themselves is an abundance magnet.

Secondly, when a Projector learns to trust the abundant trajectory of the universe and can wait comfortably for the right invitation to arrive, they conserve their precious energy. Projectors can feel vibrant, vital and ready for the invitations when they manifest. Burned out Projectors, on the other hand, sometimes have to turn down good invitations if they've wasted their energy pursuing something that isn't correct for them.

When a Projector is living their wealth theme, they are serving as "midwives" to the world. They guide, coach and nurture others into fulfilling their roles as initiators and builders. Projectors truly tend to the template of the evolution of the world in every aspect. When Projectors are serving in this capacity, they are strong and powerful blessings to the world around them. They are magnets for abundant opportunities.

When Projectors first learn their strategy of waiting for invitations, they often have to dramatically align their current life. Sometimes Projectors have to maintain their "day job" because they need money. It can be tricky to keep the traditional flow of income and to simultaneously shift to waiting for the right thing to come to you.

It is important for Projectors to do whatever they can do to stay out of the bitterness (the emotional theme of the Projector). While they're waiting, Projectors need to stay in their joy and follow their bliss. It's not unusual for Projectors to take a deep dive into what brings them joy only to find that their next invitation is deeply aligned with the joy they've been pursuing!

Projectors are gifted at knowing others, yet not so good at knowing themselves. Sometimes a Projector will benefit from having a good friend not because they need advice, but because they have to see their decisions in the context of someone else in order for them to know what is right for themselves. Talking helps a Projector "see" themselves and can be crucial to help them get clarity before making big decisions.

Self-care, rest, restoration, working on self-worth and self-value are the most important things Projectors can do to activate their abundance blueprint. When Projectors feel energized and valuable, they transform not only their loved ones and themselves but ultimately the world around them.

**Reflector Type**

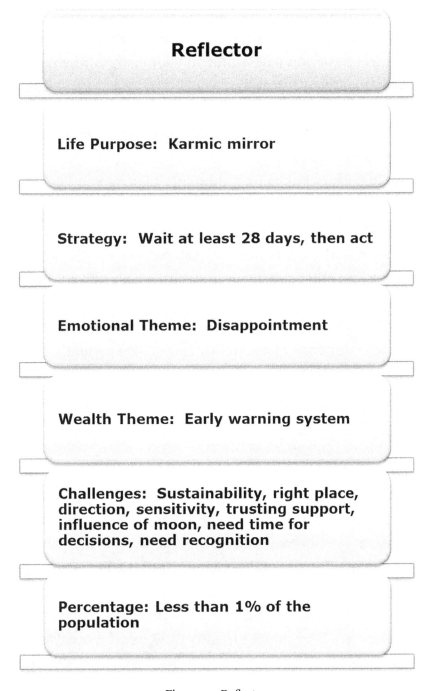

Figure 43. Reflector

The Reflector is the rarest of all the five Types. The Reflector also has the most unique and deliberate strategy.

When you look at a Reflector chart, all of the Centers in the chart are white. Remember that wherever you have white on your chart is where you receive and amplified energy from the world around you.

Reflectors receive every kind of energy possible from the people and the community around them. That means that at any given point in time, a Reflector is experiencing everyone else's energies.

That means Reflectors are feeling, thinking, sensing and knowing everything that is going on around them on a deep, experiential level. And, while that gives the Reflector tremendous potential for awareness of what's up in their world, a Reflector who doesn't understand their hardwiring can feel confused, lost, overwhelmed, struggle with direction and consistency and have a very difficult time figuring out what to do to create abundance in their life.

The purpose of a Reflector is to serve as a "karmic mirror" for their community. A Reflector has the role of reflecting back to the people around them the health and energetic vibration of their community.

If a Reflector is happy, they are experiencing a happy community. If a Reflector is troubled, struggling or feeling full of lack, they are experiencing an unhappy community. Their sense of direction in life will always be determined by their community. Because of this, it is crucial for the Reflector to be in the right community — the community who they are designed to serve and reflect.

As you can imagine, if you are so sensitive that you are constantly experiencing the energies of others, it's difficult to connect with your own energy and feel what is good and right for you. Because of the complexity of the Reflector experience, they need three things to make abundant, authentic choices.

First, they need to in a geographical location that feels good to them. Reflectors need to love where they live and love their coworkers. If those two factors are out of alignment, a Reflector will feel stuck or trapped and their abundance flow will feel stagnant.

Secondly, Reflectors need time... lots of time. It takes time for a Reflector to sort out everyone else's energy amidst their own. Not only that, a Reflector is deeply impacted by the movement of the moon through their chart, changing the nature of their own energy over the course of 28 days. Reflectors need at least 28 days to wait and feel their way into making good decisions.

Thirdly, because Reflectors have very little consistent energy inside of themselves, they need relationships that "reflect" their own decision-making process. A Reflector has to talk through their decisions aloud and see their choices "reflected" through others in conversation, much like a Projector.

Reflectors, like Manifestors and Projectors, do not have consistent energy for working. Although a Reflector can experience enormous amounts of energy from others and can be tremendously powerful, their energy is not consistent or sustainable. Because of this, traditional jobs can be difficult for the Reflector to maintain without regular cycles of rest and restoration.

You can imagine if you are not designed to work, need a minimum of 28 days and lots of conversations to make a good decision for yourself that it's hard for the Reflector to tap into their abundance flow if they don't understand their very unique hard-wiring.

In my limited experience of Reflectors, I've found that many Reflectors seem to craft a lifestyle where they are lovingly supported by others. Reflectors can love and feel deeply; they have the ability to know the full potential of what it means to live in community together and to experience all that it means to be human. They bear witness to the human process and potential.

This can be beautiful but also disappointing for the Reflector, especially if they are in the wrong community. The disappointment of the Reflector can cause them to turn away from the world and from serving as the powerful barometers of their community that they are serving.

Reflectors can also experience deep disappointment about their own personal choices. When they don't know to wait and talk through their decisions with others, Reflectors can make hasty decisions that don't turn out like they expect. This can make it traumatic for Reflectors to not only trust themselves, but also the abundant nature of life and in their ability to tap into a prosperous life.

The world isn't really set up for a Reflector. The challenge of feeling pressured to make fast decisions can deeply impair the Reflectors own natural process of aligning with what's right and abundant for them. Reflectors need time and a supportive community. The most important thing for a Reflector is to find their right place and to take their time getting there.

## The Sacral Types: The Pure Generators and the Manifesting

### Generators

There are two different kinds of Generator Types: the pure Generator and the Manifesting Generator. Manifesting Generators are a mix of some of the themes of the Generator and a handful of themes from the Manifestor. But, overall, the Manifesting Generator is first and foremost a Generator Type.

## The Pure Generator Type

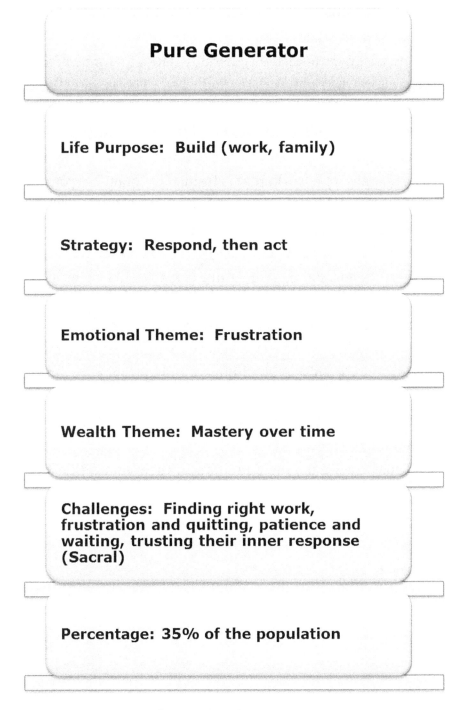

**Pure Generator**

**Life Purpose:** Build (work, family)

**Strategy:** Respond, then act

**Emotional Theme:** Frustration

**Wealth Theme:** Mastery over time

**Challenges:** Finding right work, frustration and quitting, patience and waiting, trusting their inner response (Sacral)

**Percentage:** 35% of the population

Figure 44. Pure Generator Type

Generator Types have a life purpose of building and doing the work of the world. The ultimate goal of a Generator is to find the work they love and to dedicate their life and energy to fulfilling that calling.

But, it can be tricky because the Generator doesn't so much "find" the right work as much as allows the right work to "find" them. This is a small, but vital, shift in perspective that can make the difference between a masterful and abundant life or a life filled with false starts, unmet expectations and frustration.

The Generator Strategy is to wait to respond to what life brings to them. That sounds strangely passive to a world that is trained to "manifest your destiny," but for all Types except the Manifestor, going out and forcing the world to bend to their desires simply does not work.

The Generator flow of abundance is activated when they pay attention to the "signs" the universe sends. Being a Generator is kind of like being a detective who follows life's clues that show the way and which direction to take next.

Not only do Generators follow clues, whatever the Generator chooses to follow has to feel good and right. Too often we believe that to create what we want in life requires suffering, compromise and a litany of doing things we don't want to do (or that we are taught we "should" do). For Generators (and all humans), following what feels obligated and stiff is the fastest route to burning out, which leads to pushing wealth (and joy) away.

Generator Types have a unique definition in their charts that makes them a Generator Type — they are the only Types that have a defined Sacral Energy Center.

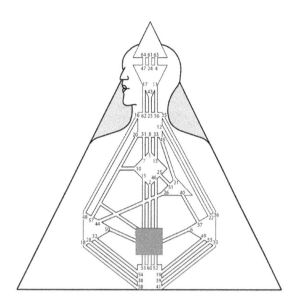

Figure 45. Sacral Energy Center

The Sacral is the energy Center for work and sexuality. Because for Generators the Sacral is always "defined," it means that Generators have consistent energy for work as well as all of the expressions of sexuality (including the energy to provide and to raise children to adulthood).

Response is how the Sacral Center works. Even though it is the most powerful energy Center in the Human Design Body Graph, it is an energy that dances with life. You can't push when you have a defined Sacral. You can only wait to see what life brings you and then respond to it.

That sounds like a lot of waiting for a high energy Type of person, but actually, Generators have the opportunity to respond to life every day. They respond to what to eat, what to wear, what to do, who to do it with and when it comes to abundance, what kind of work to do.

Generator Types hear life talking to them through "signs." It can be something as simple as a postcard with a scene from a beautiful beach that inspires them to vacation at a tropical island… it can be a license plate from a city that they want to visit… it can be a phone call or an advertisement for something they want.

When the Generator bumps into a sign that life is sending them, there is a definite response. They have a deep, non-verbal, gut-level reaction that sounds like "uh-huh" for "yes" and "unh-unh" for "no." This is a speedy internal Sacral response bypasses the noise and "shoulds" of the mind because it is the compass for the direction a Generator should follow.

But, learning how to trust your Sacral response is difficult and requires that you surrender the belief that "reasoning" and being "reasonable" is the best way to create success and abundance. Truth is, if "reasoning" was such an effective tool for creating abundance, most of us wouldn't be struggling.

For Generators, the Sacral response is how they tune into the flow of abundance. If Generators follow that deep inner knowingness and give themselves permission to do what feels good and juicy instead of what they think is "right," they will align themselves with sustainable abundance, the right work and deep fulfillment in a very short time.

The emotional theme for Generators is frustration. Failure to understand the role that frustration plays as part of the Generator experience causes many Generators to quit just prior to having a breakthrough.

Generators have a stair-step learning curve (versus the standard progressive learning curve that we all think is the signature of having made a successful decision). There is no linear progress for Generators.

When they respond to a new situation in life, Generators have an initial surge in mastery. Things move quickly and seem satisfying in addition to being fun. But, it's a normal part of the Generator process to have a cycle of sitting on a plateau where nothing seems to be happening.

These plateaus are a crucial part of the Generator process. During a plateau phase, Generators are given a chance to rest, study, explore and feel their way into what may be coming next. They may feel like inertia but they are, in fact, in the cycle where energy is building for the next opportunity.

Inertia cycles inspire frustration in Generators (and frustration and anger for Manifesting Generators). Instead of waiting out the inertia, most Generators quit in frustration and never have the opportunity to experience the next surge in mastery. They miss the opportunity to experience a deeper expression of their life calling and right work.

It is these cycles of inertia that give the Generator their greatest wealth challenge. The wealth theme of the Generator is to become masterful at whatever they have chosen as the "suggestion" that needs response. Most Generators get frustrated when they hit their plateau of inertia and many quit before the next surge in mastery. This denies them the blessing and opportunity of experiencing whatever it is they are here to build in the world.

To align with true abundance, the Generators have to learn to wait and also manage their frustration in healthy and dynamic ways so that they can be masters in life.

**Manifesting Generator Type**

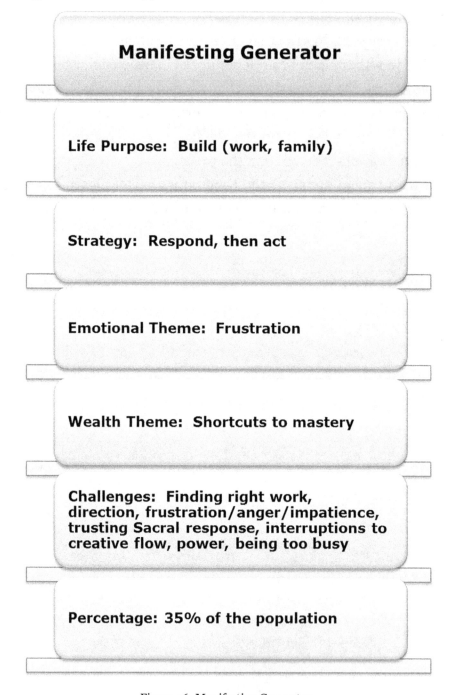

Figure 46. Manifesting Generator

Manifesting Generators are essentially the same as pure Generators with a couple of small differences.

First of all, the Manifesting Generator also has a defined Sacral, like the pure Generator but there is something different; they will also have at least one channel that connects one (or more) motor Center (the Sacral, the Will, the Emotional Solar Plexus and the Root Center) to the Throat Center.

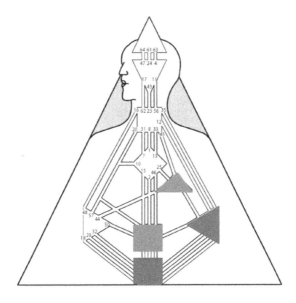

Figure 47. Motor Centers

The effect of this additional energy to the Throat Center means that a Manifesting Generator can respond very quickly to things and also respond to more than one thing at a time.

To stay healthy and in alignment with their wealth theme, Manifesting Generators actually need to do more than one thing at a time and it's normal for them to have a "trial" period of "trying on" something that they've responded to quickly before really committing.

Once they commit, however, they will experience the same stair-step learning curve as the pure Generator but often skip steps and plateaus. This often results in the Manifesting Generator appearing to go "faster" than others but often missing important details. But, the Manifesting Generator has an additional wealth theme that the pure Generator doesn't. Manifesting Generators are designed to find shortcuts and doing things at high speed is part of their wealth theme.

Sometimes people think that Manifesting Generators are "better" than pure Generators because they are faster initially. But, much like the tortoise and the hare, the Manifesting Generator will lose time responding to opportunities to repair their mistakes or the steps they've skipped.

The Manifesting Generator also has some traits that are similar to the Manifestor. The Manifesting Generator has similar internal, non-verbal creative flow. Because of this, they often struggle to ask for help and react with frustrated anger when their flow is interrupted.

Like the Manifestor Type, Manifesting Generators also need to make sure they are informing others who will be impacted by their actions so they can prepare for the wave of energy that is the Manifesting Generator. And, just like the Manifestor, the Manifesting Generator is not here to stop their creative flow or to be told what to do.

For the Manifesting Generator to stay aligned with their abundance, they need to respond to the right work, "try on" their response to see how it feels and then jump into the process of manifesting their many creative flows.

## Human Design Type Worksheet

**My Type:**_____

---

**My Type's Life Purpose:**_____

How aligned do I feel with my Life Purpose?

What's missing in my alignment with my Life Purpose?

What could I do to support more alignment with my Life's Purpose?


**My Type's Strategy:**_____

How aligned do I feel with my Strategy?

What's missing in my alignment with my Strategy?

What could I do to support more alignment with my Strategy?


What % of time do I experience my Not-Self Theme of:

_____? _____%

What could I do that would reduce my experience of my Not-Self Theme?


**My Type's Wealth Theme:**_____

How aligned do I feel with my Wealth Theme ?

What's missing in my alignment with my Wealth Theme?

How could I leverage my Wealth Theme to create more abundance in my life?

---

These are the challenges for my Type that I relate to:

_____

_____

_____

Here's how I could alleviate some or all of those challenges:_____

_____

_____

_____

---

Figure 48. Human Design Type Worksheet

## Human Design Action Summary

Please go back and read all your answers so far. Identify two or three actions you would like to implement that really resonate with you and list them here:

1)

2)

3)

Figure 49. Human Design Action Summary

# Karen Curry Parker

# The Nine Centers and Abundance

Living true to your Human Design Type is, by far, the most important part of creating abundance in your life. If you only do one thing - and that one thing is to live true to your Human Design Type - you will begin to experience a completely different level of alignment and abundance in your life.

While living your Type is the simplest way to tap into your abundance blueprint, understanding more subtle areas of your energetic hard-wiring can speed up the process of living true to your authentic self. Your nine energy Centers influence the way you think and feel, and knowing how your configuration "works" gives you powerful insights — rationale into why you've made past choices and gives you ways to newly leverage your energy so that you are more conscious and deliberate in what you choose to create in your life.

There are nine energy Centers in the Human Design chart. Each Center is responsible for processing specific kinds of energies. In addition, how you use and experience these energies is influenced by which Centers you have "open" (white) and "defined" (colored).

Open Centers take in energy in an amplified way. Because of this, wherever you have open Centers in your chart, you will be "imprinted" by other people's energies. This "imprinting" can create predictable belief and behavior challenges. If you don't understand how your energy system operates, it can diminish what is truth for you and, of course, take away from the authentic expression of your abundance.

Understanding your open Centers can really help you see different events and areas of your life. For instance, you may gain clarity as to why and how you may feel stuck in your life, why you've made the decisions you've made, the motivations that drive you in your choices and how you can leverage your open Centers instead of allowing your energy to be "hijacked" by others.

Each Center has a specific theme and a specific unconscious motivation that "kicks in" when you aren't aware of how your open Centers work. When you become conscious of how your energy Centers function, you can begin to use your openness to deeply understand others, assess the energy around you and make wise choices that are rooted in what is authentic and abundant for you, without defaulting to old patterns that may not even belong to you.

In this chapter, you will be given a brief overview of each Center, how the open Center theme of each Center may be affecting your abundance consciousness and some exercises to help you get clearer about how you have been imprinted by other people's energies. (If you'd like to learn even more about the nine Centers, I invite you to check out my book, *Understanding Human Design, The New Science of Astrology: Discover Who You Really Are.*)

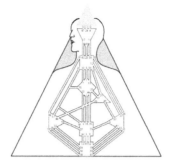

Figure 50. Head Center

**Open Head Center**

Inspiration and ideas

Pressure to figure things out

Influenced by ideas of others

Use Strategy to know which ideas to choose

**Question for the Open Head Center:**

Am I trying to fulfill someone else's inspiration? Am I under pressure to figure things out? Do I trust that the answers that I seek will be revealed to me? Am I allowing myself to dream and stay in wonder?

**Affirmation for the Open Head Center:**

I am deeply inspired all the time. I am wise about what is truly inspiring. I follow my Strategy to help me decide what I need to do. The questions in my head are from others. I don't have to answer all of them, only the ones that truly excite me!

**Affirmations for My Defined Head Center:**

I am inspired and inspiring. I spread inspiration everywhere I go and I share my ideas and inspirations with others.

Figure 51. Head Center Energies and Affirmations

The Head Center is for ideas and inspirations. Most of us have this Center open. We receive inspiration from the forces and energies around us; the Head Center takes this inspiration and translates it into questions of wonder and possibility.

The Head Center has three primary questions: how, what if and can this be true? When we get inspired, we are not designed to have answers to our inspiration, only questions. The purpose of the Head Center is to imagine and dream about possibilities, not to figure things out.

But, not trying to figure things out is tricky because the Head Center is a pressure Center. When we get inspired, most of us get under pressure to find the answers to the questions that inspiration triggers.

When we don't understand that this "force" is the pressure to dream (not the pressure to "do"), we mistakenly leap into action trying. We want to make the manifestation of an inspiration or a thought a reality. This often results in the expenditure of a lot of energy with little results. True inspiration comes from outside of us in the material world, not from our minds.

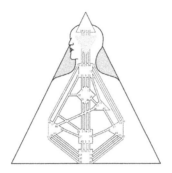

Figure 52. Ajna Center

**Open Ajna**

Designed to be open minded

Unlimited perspectives

Wise about data and analysis

Struggles with certainty

May struggle to remember data

**Questions for the Open Ajna:**

In what areas am I struggling for certainty? Are my beliefs serving me? Is it okay for me to think about things from many perspectives? Can I stay joyfully engaged in the realm of possibility?

**Affirmation for the Open Ajna:**

I am wise about information and beliefs. My gift is that I can see many sides of an issue and have many different understandings that are fluid and that change all the time. I don't have to make up my mind. I always write down the things I want to remember.

**Affirmations for My Defined Ajna Center:**

I am gentle with my thinking and always remember that there are many ways to think about information. I am uniquely capable of being certain. I listen carefully to the thoughts of others and allow for limitless thinking with grace.

Figure 53. Ajna Center Energies and Affirmations

The Ajna Center is the Center for processing and analyzing information. This is where we store thoughts, concepts and belief systems.

Again, most people will have this Center open; when this Center is open, it is beautifully designed to understand information and beliefs from multiple perspectives. Consequently, people who have this Center open are often under pressure to hold onto fixed ideas and beliefs so that they can feel "certain" about information.

Of course, the irony is that there is no certainty in the open Ajna Center. It's simply not designed that way.

We have been trained that our thoughts become things, that our thinking creates our reality. We have also learned that if we want to create what we really want in life, we have to hold onto that "vision" and never waiver with our certainty, maintaining focus on what we want.

When you can understand that most of us literally cannot hold onto a fixed idea or "vision," it starts to make sense why so many people get stuck trying to use their mind (or thought forms) to create.

If we look at the Gates located in the Head and the Ajna, the two Centers associated with thinking and mindset, we see that the energies in the mind are comprised of the potential for confusion, overwhelm, doubt and suspicion as well as false answers, rationalization, oppressive thinking, opinions, thoughts that are difficult to share and ideas that have no energy to be made manifest.

**Gates and Channels of Head and Ajna**

**64-47 Confusion; possibilities**

**61-24 Daydreaming/thinking**

**63-4 Doubt, logic, answers**

**17-62 Opinions and details**

**43-23 Insights, new thinking**

**11-56 Ideas and stories**

Figure 54. Gate and Channels for Head and Ajna

When looking at it this way, we can see the Head and Ajna are not good places for making decisions! Here is a list of parallels for these two Centers:

- pressure when open; fixed when defined
- no energy for action; mental
- confusion, thinking, doubt
- mindset, justifications, answers (even if wrong)
- opinions, insights, ideas
- details, not listening, stories

When we look at the mechanics of how the mind operates and the process of manifesting, we see that there are two key roles that the mind plays:

1. The mind is designed to use questioning as the "interface" between the human experience and the infinite possibilities of the universe. We are designed to ask questions and receive answers from our outer reality, not to use the mind to force answers and figure out what to "do."

2. The dreaming and imaginative capacity of the mind is designed to stimulate a "mindset" that attunes the rest of the energy system to attract what you want in your life. And, because the role of the mind *is* attunement, rather than to create, you don't have to figure everything out (the universe takes care of that for you).

Learning to use the mind the way it is intended allows you to leverage your creative wonder, uncertainty and the realm of possibility in a way that liberates you from having to control your mind in unnatural ways.

To really get what you want in life, you must become a master of your mindset. You do this by allowing yourself to engage in creative questions and dreaming rather than to try to force yourself to hold onto a fixed vision or belief in an unnatural way.

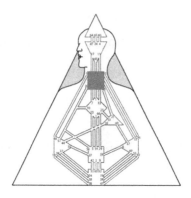

Figure 55. Throat Center

**The Open Throat Center**

Speaks for others; modulates

Wise about communication

Needs recognition to be heard

Recognition can drive decisions

May push to be heard, burn out

Patterns of inappropriate ways to get attention; pressure to speak

**Questions for the Open Throat Center:**

Are my actions motivated by a need for attention and recognition? Am I pushing with energy that I don't have?

**Affirmations for My Open Throat Center:**

My words are heard best when I am invited to speak. I save my words for people who truly desire to hear my point of view and insights. I wait for the right people to ask me and value my words.

**Affirmations for My Defined Throat Center:**

I speak with great responsibility and know the true source of my words. I allow others to have a voice and I use my words to invite others to share.

Figure 56. Throat Center Energies and Affirmations

The Throat Center is the Center for communication and manifestation into action. In the Human Design Chart, the Throat Center is more like a gearbox and regulates, to a certain degree, the rest of the Chart.

The Throat Center translates ideas and possibilities as well as gives energy for "doing" into words. Words ground us and anchor us in the earthly world, making it easier for us to communicate ideas about what needs to be done with each other.

In the Hebrew language, the word for "word" and the word for "thing" are the same word. Things do not become "things" until we can define them with words. You can see the tremendous creative potential in the Throat Center when you understand this.

If Human Design was a game, the name of the game would be to get as much energy as possible to the Throat Center. Manifestors and Manifesting Generators have a motor (Sacral, Will, Emotional Solar Plexus or the Root) connected to their Throat Center via a defined Channel. When you have a motor to your Throat, you can initiate conversations and certain actions in the way that's right for your Human Design Type.

Generators, Projectors and Reflectors do not have motors connected to their Throat Centers. That means that they need to get their energy for manifesting from their connections with other people. In other words, Generators, Projectors and Reflectors are people "who need people" to get things done in the world.

(Quick tip: If you are a Generator, Projector or Reflector and you feel like you're struggling to get something done, you can often benefit from the collective aura of places like coffee shops, because in those kinds of places, you can "pick" up the energy of others and get more power for doing connected to your Throat Center.)

Whatever Center gets connected to your Throat Center will determine a lot about how you perceive yourself and what you like to discuss. If you are a Generator, Projector or Reflector, since you don't have the capacity to initiate the way Manifestors and Manifesting Generators do, you may find that you can sometimes feel like no one hears you.

Having a non-motorized Throat Center means that you do best in conversations and interactions where other people give you something to respond to or ask you a question first.

This is even truer if you have an open Throat Center. When you have an open Throat Center, you are here to be wise about communication. You have the capacity to modulate the way you talk and share information with others based on their design. An open Throat gives you a lot of variability in how you communicate with others.

But to be heard with an open Throat Center, you have to be recognized or asked. If you have an open Throat and you are not waiting to be asked, you run the risk of spending a lot of energy trying to get attention so you can be heard. Then, even when you're heard, you run the risk of people not really understanding what you're saying.

Let's look at this in the context of the traditional "success formula" that we are taught from an early age. In school, we are trained that to be successful in life you have to "grab the bull by the horns" and "the early bird gets the worm" and you can "manifest your destiny" by "pulling yourself up by your own bootstraps."

All nice concepts for Manifestors and Manifesting Generators, but for the rest of humanity (and especially those of you with open Throats), to try to force your success in this style only results in you using a lot of energy you don't have and then feeling invisible in the world.

In addition, because a non-motorized Throat Center needs to be recognized or given something to respond to be heard, Generators, Projectors and Reflectors are often motivated by a need to seek attention. That means that sometimes they give up what they truly want and do things that they think others will notice or like. This kind of motivation makes it difficult to align with your authentic desires because the need for attention overrides what you really need and want.

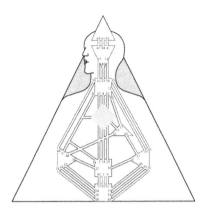

Figure 57. G-Center aka Identity Center

**Open G-Center (aka Identity Center)**
Fluid, adaptable, chameleon
"Right place; right people"
Wise about love, life directions
Question lovability; struggle with direction and sense of self
Decision-making issues: while conditioned, need auric space
to disconnect from others' identities and directions

**Questions for the Open G-Center:**
Am I in the right place? Does my environment support me?
Am I surrounded by people who inspire me to fulfill my
authentic desires? Do I feel lovable? Am I motivated by a
need to show my love-worthiness? Am I trying to lock myself
into a direction that doesn't feel right?

**Affirmations for My Open G-Center:**
How I experience myself changes depending on who is around
me. I choose to surround myself with people who feel good to
me. Place is very important to me and I create an
environment that soothes me. When I am in the right place,
the right opportunities come to me.

**Affirmations for My Defined G-Center:**
I am who I am. I express myself in all that I do. I celebrate
the magnificence of who I am.

Figure 58. G-Center Energies and Affirmations

The G-Center is the Center for love and direction in the chart. It is a key Center for creating abundance in your life because the G-Center contains the mechanics for the Law of Attraction.

Contained within the G-Center is a magnetic monopole. A magnetic monopole is a magnet that has only one pole and only attracts. We never push abundance away. We only attract to the degree to which we are energetically attuned to our abundance.

Scientists are now able to actually measure a magnetic resonance field around the heart in the body. The heart is partially located in the G-Center. I believe that as we do more research in this area that we will discover even more deeply the magnetic or attractive powers of the heart.

Your level of abundance is determined by the eight energies located on the G-Center, which are:

1. Self-Love
2. Empowerment
3. Alignment with your authentic self
4. The lessons you've learned from the past
5. Your alignment with Spirit
6. Embodiment and body image
7. Your capacity to allow and receive
8. Your service to the greater good

These eight energies are derived from the eight Gates located on the G-Center.

The bottom line to attracting abundance is this: You will attract into your life experiences that will teach you how to love yourself, be powerful, express yourself authentically, let go of and learn from the past, how to surrender and trust a spiritual force that is bigger than your individual self, love and take care of your body, how to trust (and allow) the universal abundant flow of life and to make choices that, not only take care of yourself, but serve humanity.

When we are out of alignment with any of these energies, our magnetic monopole will attract into our lives opportunities and lessons that are designed to teach us how to be more in alignment with who we really are: powerful, loving, abundant beings.

If you're not experiencing what you want in your life and you feel like your abundance magnet is "broken" or that the Law of Attraction doesn't work for you, it may be that the infinite and abundant wisdom of the universe is bringing you the exact experience you need to master yourself.

We often talk about the mind/body connection and the importance of integrating the two. Physiologists and neurologists are discovering that there is a surprising connection between the digestive system, the heart and the mind. The Vagus nerve connects all three of these key parts of the body.

In the Human Design chart, we see a profound energy connection between the mind, the emotions (which are located in the gut) and the heart. The nexus of manifesting is the G-Center. The energy of the mind and the vibration of the Emotional Solar Plexus tune the magnetic force in the G-Center and cause you to attract into your life experiences that are in tune with your G-Center.

When the G-Center is open, it makes it more challenging to harmonize your attraction power with what is authentic to you. An open G-Center will take in the direction and identity of others in a deep and sensitive way. The beauty and wisdom of this openness is that when the G-Center is open there is the potential for tremendous wisdom about love, direction and about others. But, if you don't understand that your own destiny, identity and direction can be energetically deeply influenced by the people around you, it can make it very difficult for you to find your right direction in life.

The open G-Center has the potential to go in many, many directions in life. It's supposed to do that.

Imagine that life is like a restaurant. The defined G-Center can eat at the Restaurant of Life and order off the menu because there is a fixed selection or potential for direction for the defined G-Center. The open G-Center goes to the Restaurant of Life and selects menu options from the mega buffet because there are endless choices when you have an open G-Center. The right choices are determined by following your Human Design strategy for your Type.

Geography can also help align the direction of the open G-Center. When the G-Center is open, being in the right geographical location can help you attract what you want in your life. The open G-Center has to feel good where you are. When you love where you live and love who you are with, life works. If someone with an open G-Center feels stuck or like nothing is moving in their life, it might be that they are in the wrong place or with the wrong people.

Because the underlying motivation of the open G-Center is to question their love-worthiness, an open G-Center person sometimes makes choices to prove their lovability. That means they can get into patterns of doing things that they don't really want to do in order to "keep" someone's love.

In addition, because an open G-Center feels other people's identities deeply, it's easy to take on someone else's identity and lose yourself and your direction in other people. Taking time alone and away from other people's energy can help the open G-Center recalibrate back to their authentic direction.

To create true and lasting abundance when you have an open G-Center, you have to accept that your life will naturally take you in many directions and that you have to be in the right place with the right people to make things work. When all of these factors line up and you love yourself deeply, your G-Center naturally attracts into your life experiences and abundance that reflects the love that is you.

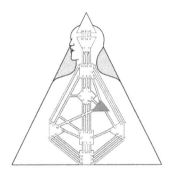

Figure 59. Will Center

**Open Will Center**

Wise about value, business, managing material resources

Amplifies Will Power of others

Questions value of self

Needs to prove oneself

Do not make promises

**Questions for the open Will Center:**

Do I value myself? Am I taking care of myself? Do I trust the universe enough to rest and resource myself? Am I pushing too hard? Am I burned out? Do I need to nurture myself first before I move forward? What am I trying to prove?

**Affirmation for the open Will Center:**

I enter into all agreements according to my Human Design Strategy. I make promises and commitments very carefully and deliberately, only according to my Human Design Strategy. I have nothing to prove and I value myself deeply. I fearlessly ask to be paid what I am worth.

**Affirmations for My Defined Will Center:**

It is important for me to rest. Rest allows me to recharge my willpower. I honor the promises that I make. I make deliberate promises and understand that people expect me to keep my promises. I am gentle with my expectations of others. Not everyone can just do the things that I do.

Figure 60. Will Center Energies and Affirmations

The Will Center is the Center that is most closely associated with money. The Will Center is the Center for will power and gives us the energy to push to create resources. It also gives us the energy to endure when things are tough and the capacity to convert ideas and information into money. It is a vital part of the circuitry in the chart that is associated with business, budgeting, money and (ironically) spirituality.

The other irony of the Will Center is that 7/8 of the people on the planet do not have consistent willpower, yet we are obsessed with it and have a tendency to beat ourselves up if we don't have it.

If you don't have willpower you are not weak nor do you have some kind of personality flaw. You are normal.

The Will Center is a motor and consequently has power. But another irony of the Will Center is that the full capacity of this energy Center isn't activated until we surrender to Source. In other words, if you let go and value yourself enough to nurture and take care of yourself and trust that you'll have all that you need, you'll activate a lot more energy than if you use your human will and push hard.

The Will Center is designed to work and also to rest. The purpose of the resting cycle of willpower is to re-Source yourself so that you can create more resources. The metaphor of the Will Center is told beautifully in the Old Testament. When the Israelites escape slavery and are wandering in the desert, they are worried and afraid because they have no food. God tells the people not to worry that He will provide for the People every day by giving them a special food called Manna. The people do not have to do anything to create or make the Manna. They simply need to go and gather it each day.

They are instructed not to take more than their share and, if someone is unable to gather their share, they are to bring the Manna to the person in need. In addition, God tells the people that on the sixth day of each week, they will be given an extra share of Manna to eat on the seventh day, which is to be a day of rest and reconnection with God.

This is the story of the story of the Will Center. We are designed to receive all of the resources we need and to have enough to rest and restore ourselves before we go out and create again.

There are two factors that influence how we effectively use this energy. First of all, we have to trust in the infinite supply of the universe relax into the knowing that when we rest, we will still be supported and when we emerge from rest, we will have more energy to create.

Secondly, we have to value ourselves enough to nurture and take care of ourselves so that we can better fulfill our destinies and be capable of doing the work we need to do in order to turn ideas into resources.

Because the Will Center is directly connected to both the Emotional Solar Plexus and the G-Center, it is part of the vagal nerve/ mind-body-heart connection that is a vital part of the creative cycle. How much you value money, work, your creative contribution and, most importantly, yourself influences the G-Center and the magnetic monopole and consequently what you're attracting into your life.

When you have an open Will Center, you are designed to become wise about what is truly valuable in life and we often discover that true value has nothing to do with money. In fact, research shows that the majority of people in America value freedom more than they value money.

The open Will Center is often motivated by a need to prove its value and worth. When you have an open Will Center, it's common to try to prove how hard you work to demonstrate your value. The truth is, we are all inherently valuable and you add the most value to the world (and to your work) when you value yourself enough to take care of yourself in a joyful, sustainable way.

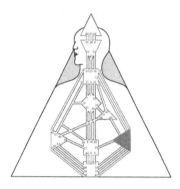

Figure 61. Emotional Solar Plexus Center

**The Open Emotional Solar Plexus**
Empathic, feels others' feelings
Wise about emotions and passion
Overwhelm, pain, confusion
Tries to keep everyone happy
Be screen not sponge, then speak your truth and handle conflict

**Questions for the open Emotional Solar Plexus:**
Am I honoring my truth and doing what I want and what is good for me? Am I compromising what I want in order to keep others happy? Am I making choices based on my desire to avoid conflict?

**Affirmation for the open Emotional Solar Plexus:**
I can make decisions in the moment. I pay attention to the source of my emotions and allow others to experience their feelings without making their experience my own. I am very sensitive and I trust my insights about other people's feelings. I take frequent breaks when the emotional energy is too intense.

**Affirmations for My Defined Solar Plexus Center:**
I take my time making decisions and know that I reach clarity over time. I am here to be deliberate, not spontaneous.

Figure 62. Emotional Solar Plexus Center Energies and Affirmations

The Emotional Solar Plexus is the Center that is truly the most creative Center in the Human Design Body Graph. It is in the Emotional Solar Plexus that we find the potential for so many things: creating intimacy and community; creative expression in the form of words, poetry, writing and music; the potential for new experiences that stretch the limits of the human experience; the possibility for peace and sustainable resources, and; alchemy and a deep connection with Spirit and abundance.

In spite of the wealth of possibilities in the Emotional Solar Plexus, we are not taught how to use this energy correctly as part of our infinite capacity to manifest. Part of the challenge is that we've mistakenly been taught that thinking and reasoning are the best ways to create. And many of us have never been taught to use the juicy, rich energy of emotions as part of the creative process.

The Emotional Solar Plexus energy operates in waves. It's a frequency of energy that has ups and downs or highs and lows. When you have a defined (colored) Emotional Solar Plexus, your natural emotional energy will vary. Because of this, you need to feel your way into your decisions and you need to give yourself time to feel what is right for you. The defined Emotional Solar Plexus is not designed to be spontaneous.

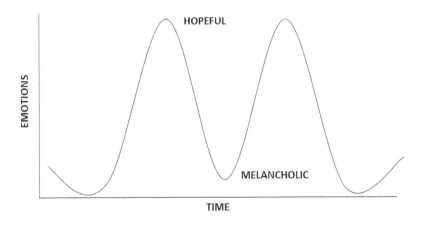

Figure 63. Emotional Wave

If you have a defined Emotional Solar Plexus, you may have a history of being disappointed with your life choices. Because you have an internal natural vibration of emotional energy that is dynamic and requires time for clarity, you may have never given yourself time to make good choices.

People with a defined Emotional Solar Plexus will tend to leap into things when they are feeling good and then be frustrated or confused when in a day or two (when their emotional energy has shifted), their enthusiasm for their decision wanes.

The secret to making good choices when you have a defined Emotional Solar Plexus is to take your time and feel your way into your choices. The more time you allow yourself, the easier it is for you to make a choice that lasts and stays consistent energetically.

The key to remember when you have this Center defined is that the choices that are right for you will feel correct *while you wait for clarity.* If you are feeling all over the place about a decision, it's probably not the right one for you.

When this Center is open, you are emphatic and feel everyone else's emotional energy in an amplified way. This makes you feel very emotionally conscious and sensitive. Your sensitivity to other people's emotions can unconsciously drive you to want to keep everyone "happy." Because you are empathic, when everyone else is happy, you feel happy and the energy in the room feels good.

While it's nice to be able to sense and anticipate everyone's needs, it makes it hard sometimes to deal with conflict and truth. It's also hard to ask for what you want, especially if you feel that your needs will cause other's to react to you. Many people with open emotional energy will avoid truth and conflict and give up what they want in the name of keeping everyone else happy.

Compromising what you want and need does not create abundance. In fact, because we are all designed to be abundant if you are actively avoiding what you want or need because you think it's inconvenient for others or may cause an emotional "wave," you will begin to push abundance away on every level. Compromise is never a good strategy, especially when it comes to getting what you need and want.

Emotionally open people have to learn how to feel the energy in the room, assess it, realize that it's not personal, stop taking responsibility for it and muster up the courage to ask for what they need. It can be a lifelong challenge, but vital if you want to fully claim the abundance that is waiting for you.

It's important to understand how your Emotional Solar Plexus is defined, but there is one other important factor we have to consider when we look at Emotional energy to determine how it is vital to the process of creating wealth and abundance.

The Emotional Solar Plexus is the Center for the most creative energy in the Human Design chart. It is the frequency of energy that regulates the magnetic monopole (the Law of Attraction mechanism located in the G-Center). Mastering your Emotional energy, whether you have a defined or open Emotional Solar Plexus, is the biggest challenge of becoming an alchemist and creating what you truly want in your life.

The purpose of the Emotional Solar Plexus is to attune or set the frequency of attraction in the magnetic monopole. The vibrational frequency of the Emotional Solar Plexus synchronizes the magnetic monopole. This synchronization then causes the magnetic monopole to attract into your life opportunities and experiences that match the frequency you have set.

In other words, you attract things into your life that are in alignment with your emotional energy. We are trained to react emotionally to life and also identify with our feelings. Our vocabulary reflects these ideas. We say "I am" sad, happy, angry, etc. When you understand the Human Design chart, you will discover that the Center for the energy of "I am" is located in the G-Center and does not have nearly the volatility and mutability of the Emotional Solar Plexus.

We are not our emotions. We feel emotions, whether we are defined or open in the Emotional Solar Plexus. You can attune the quality and the character of your emotional energy by using your mind to stimulate the emotions you desire to create what you want.

We are trained to use the mind to think and figure things out. As we've seen, this doesn't really work that way in the Head and the Ajna Centers, the two Centers that comprise what we think of as "the mind." The true purpose of your mind is to stimulate your Emotional Solar Plexus to feel what you want to feel in your life by using your imagination, curiosity and your sense of wonder.

Our dreams and thoughts stimulate emotions. Those emotions, which are simply a frequency of energy, attune the G-Center and the magnetic monopole. When they are harmonized, it attracts things into your life that are vibrationally aligned with your emotional frequency.

It's a simple, albeit not always easy, formula for creating. When you can master the use of your mind, your emotions and then trust the natural unfolding of the expressions of these energies, you will be very easily and nicely aligned with your abundance.

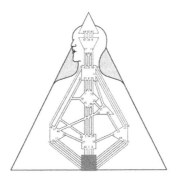

Figure 64. Root Center

**Open Root Center**
Feels pressure to get things done
Wise about pressure and stress
Can feel stressed by this energy
Struggles to be free from To-Do lists
Possible adrenal burn out
May become adrenaline junkie

**Questions for the Open Root Center:**
Am I choosing this because of the pressure? Is pressure keeping me from doing what I really want? What's the worst thing that will happen if you don't do this right now? What are you under pressure to do?

**Affirmations for My Open Root Center:**
I set realistic goals. I make powerful decisions about being free and know that things will get done when they get done. I use pressure to create more energy and at the end of the day, I rest and relax even if my "to-do" list is long. I make decisions according to my Human Design strategy even if I feel pressure. I breathe and relax knowing there is an abundance of time to get things done.

**Affirmations for My Defined Root Center:**
I honor my root pulse and wait for the energy to get things done. I get more done when the energy is "on." When the energy is off, I know that it is my time to rest and restore myself.

Figure 65. Root Center Energies and Affirmations

The Root Center is the center for adrenaline energy. It is also a pressure center. When it is open, you are under to pressure to "do" things and the pressure doesn't ease until you do it. People with open Root Centers are often leaping from thing to thing trying to get out from the pressure to "do."

When the open Root Center is used properly, it can give you a surge of energy for doing limited projects or tasks. It's just the right amount of energy to get something done.

But if you are succumbing to the pressure of the open Root Center and you are struggling with non-abundant beliefs and not trusting in the infinite supply of the universe, you're likely to be leaping into choices that you "hope" will bring you money. Get rich quick schemes and compromising on your true desires are often hallmarks of the open Root Center.

In addition, when you have an open Root Center, it's easy to feel pressure from others (even if that's not what's really happening) and you compromise what you really want in order to keep other people happy. The pressure from your open Root Center can cause you to do whatever it takes to not feel the perceived pressure from others.

The defined Root Center operates in pulses. It brings energy in cycles. For most of us with defined Root Centers operating in the traditional world, we don't have the blessing of being able to follow the natural pulse and flow of our energy. But we do usually have the energy to push even of our Root pulse is skewed. Usually, the defined Root Center has little effect on our abundance.

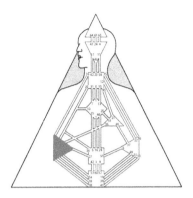

Figure 66. Spleen Center

**Open Spleen Center**

Sensitive to immune system

May struggle with being on time

Wise about health, healing, time

May be medical intuitive

Holds on to things, people, etc. for longer than should

Fears of the Spleen; move through

**Questions for the Open Spleen Center:**

Am I holding on to things, people, beliefs and/or circumstances for longer than is good for me? Is fear keeping me from fulfilling my destiny and my abundance?

**Affirmations for My Open Spleen Center:**

I easily let go of all things that do not serve my highest good. I honor my body and the messages it sends me. When I feel sick, I rest. I honor my own sense of timing and know that whenever I arrive is just perfect! I respect other people's sense of time and always wear a watch. I trust my intuition and know that I receive intuitive insights in many different ways.

**Affirmations for My Defined Spleen Center:**

I trust my intuition. I listen to my "gut" feelings and take guided action. I listen to my body. I rest and take care of myself. I honor my sense of time. I remember that not everyone is as fast as me and I flow with Universal Timing.

Figure 67. Spleen Center Energies and Affirmations

The Spleen is the center for instinct, survival and time. The goal of the Spleen Center is to give us instinctive, in-the-moment intuitive pulses that help us stay alive. The instinctive pulses of the Spleen are very time limited and specific to circumstances and situations that may be dangerous or threatening to us.

The Spleen has a very important function. It's our alarm that tells us when we are in danger and it communicates to us via fear. When we understand this fear and use it correctly, we avoid dangerous and life-threatening circumstances. For example, it's healthy to be afraid to go into a dark cave that smells like an animal lives in it or to go into a dark alley at night.

Because the fear in the Spleen Center is designed to keep us alive and involves triggering the "flight or fight" response, it is very time limited. When we feel this kind of instinctive fear, we don't stop and contemplate whether we should run or not. We flee and figure out what was up later. The fear of the Spleen Center stops as soon as we change our circumstances and we are safe again.

All animals (including humans) have instinct. But animals don't have the same kind of consciousness (and angst!) as humans. Humans can make instinct very complex and messy. When our minds and our beliefs get entangled with our survival instincts (as they do), we become deeply afraid of things that are not life-threatening and keep ourselves paralyzed in fear that has no function and is a misuse of our survival instincts and robs us of precious energy.

We are all impacted by our Spleens, whether open or defined. The Gates around the Spleen Center deeply influence all of us. When you understand your hardwiring, you will begin to see how the specific fears Gates of our Spleen Center may be keeping you stuck in your life.

You are not doomed by your Human Design or the mechanics of how your instinct works. When you follow your Human Design Strategy and you also understand the vulnerabilities of your hard-wiring, it gives you the choice to not be victimized by your Human Design, but to consciously choose to live out a higher expression of what is in your chart.

Once you understand what's holding you back, you can begin to move through the fear and experience a breakthrough. The fears of the Spleen are very time limited and, once you push through them and "just do" whatever you need to do, the fear instantly dissipates and you realize that the fears you were experiencing weren't real at all.

Look at your Human Design chart and see which, if any, of these Gates you have defined in your chart and then use the following questions to help you find the courage to push through the potential fears of your Definition and consciously choose to experience and express the highest potential of these Gates. In addition, you can use the questions listed with each Gate to help deepen your awareness of how these energies are impacting you and what you need to do to break free from this ancient patterns that may no longer serve you.

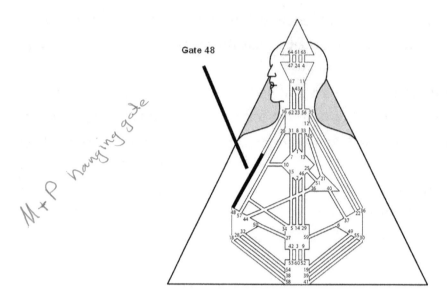

M+P hanging gate

Figure 68. Gate 48

**The Gate 48**

Low Expression: The Fear of Inadequacy

High Expression: Having deep knowledge and wisdom based on your studies and experience.

"I don't know enough. I'll never be ready."

Writing Exercise: What needs to be release or healed for me to fully express my readiness for my mastery?

Figure 69. Gate 48 Fear

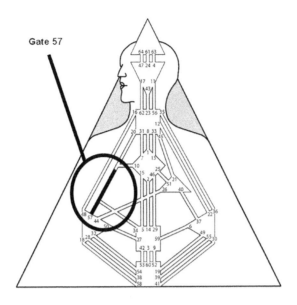

Figure 70. Gate 57

## Gate 57

Low Expression: The Fear of the Future or Fear of the Unknown

High Expression: Powerful, intuitive insights about the future.  Claircognizant.

"I'm afraid of what might happen."

Writing Exercise:  What needs to be healed or released in order for me to trust my intuition?

Figure 71. Gate 57 Fear

247

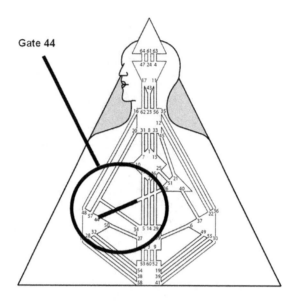

Figure 72. Gate 44

## Gate 44

Low Expression: The Fear of the Past

High Expression: The ability to see the patterns of the past and break them ensuring a better outcome.

"What if the same thing happens again?"

Writing Exercise: What pain/experiences from the past need to be released in order for me to create a different outcome and a different future?

Figure 73. Gate 44 Fear

248

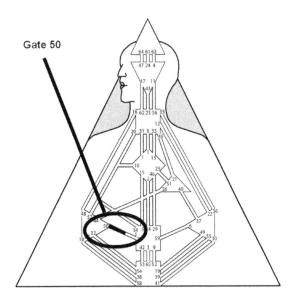

Figure 74. Gate 50

**Gate 50**

Low Expression: Fear of Failing
Everyone/Letting Others Down (The "guilt"
Gate)
High Expression: The ability to transmit and
teach important values and to nurture and
bring out the best in others.

"What if I let everyone down?"

Writing Exercise:  What actions do I need to
take or new beliefs do I need to have to
fully empower the people in my life to take
care of themselves in a healthy way?

Figure 75. Gate 50 Fear

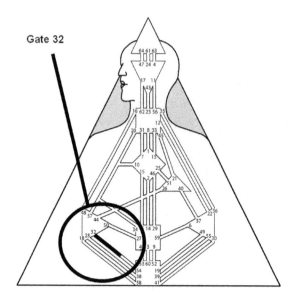

Figure 76. Gate 32

**Gate 32**

Low Expression: Fear of Failure

High Expression:  The intuition to know when the timing is right to launch a project successfully.  Patience.

"What if I do this and it doesn't work?"

Writing Exercise:  What needs to be released or healed for me to serve as a steward for my creative ideas and incubate these ideas with love and patience until the time is right to share them with the world?

Figure 77. Gate 32 Fear

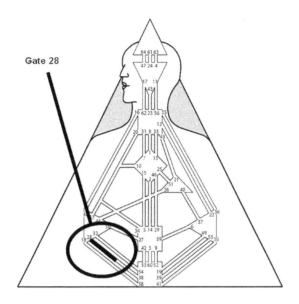

Gate 28

Figure 78. Gate 28

## Gate 28

Low Expression: Fear that it will be hard
High Expression: The joy of adventure and
challenge.

"What if the struggle of doing this exhausts
me?

Writing Exercise:  What needs to be
released/healed for me to fully embrace all
of the adventure that life is bringing me?
What needs to be released/healed for me to
allow ease in my life?

Figure 79. Gate 28 Fear

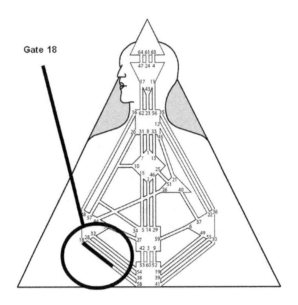

Gate 18

Figure 80. Gate 18

### Gate 18

Low Expression: Fear that it will never be right/perfect

High Expression:  The ability to correct patterns that don't work to bring people a deeper experience of mastery and joy.

"What if I put all this work into it and it's still not perfect?"

Writing Exercise:  What needs to be released/healed for me to trust that life is unfolding perfectly and that there is no such thing as "perfection"?  What love for myself do I need to have to wait patiently for people to ask me for my insights and corrections?

Figure 81. Gate 18 Fear

These energies are relevant for all of us. If you are being held hostage by your own survival instinct, push through the fear. You'll be pretty surprised at how quickly the fear goes away when you push through.

In addition, if you have an open Spleen Center, you have a tendency to hold on to your fears and things for longer than is good for you. The open Spleen tends to hold on to old stories, relationships, belongings and beliefs for longer than needed. This jams up your ability to be open to receiving and keeps you stuck in the quagmire fears of the Spleen Center. If you have an open Spleen, the challenge is for you to let go so that you can be open to allowing and receiving more.

Remember, your Human Design is not a curse. You have the power to live the highest expression of your abundance and potential when you understand how your energy is influencing you and when you live life correctly according to your Human Design Type.

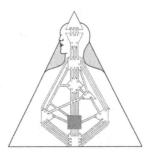

Figure 82. Sacral Center

**Open Sacral Center**
Wise about work, life, procreation
Energy not sustainable; no "work"
Can burn out if pushing
Struggles with knowing when enough is enough
May struggle with sleep; needs some alone time
May be considered "lazy" but isn't

**Questions for the Open Sacral Center:**
Do I trust Source? Do I trust that I have a "right" place in the world? Do I know when enough is enough? Do I believe that I can have money/support without "earning" it?

**Affirmations for My Open Sacral Center:**
I am not here to work in the traditional way. I can work hard in short bursts and then I need alone time to discharge the extra energy I carry. I recognize that my energy is mutable, and I take care of myself and let go of the expectations of others. I am very powerful when I am using my energy correctly.

**Affirmations for My Defined Sacral Center:**
I wait with grace and patience knowing that the right opportunities will show up for me. All I have to do is respond to the world and I will joyfully do the right work and be with the right people. I fearlessly honor my response and know that I am internally driven to be in the right place at the right time, doing the right work.

Figure 83. Sacral Center Energies and Affirmations

The Sacral Center is the center for work force and life force energy. It is the most powerful Center in the Body Graph. The defined Sacral Center is the defining energy that makes a Generator and a Manifesting Generator Type. If you have a defined Sacral Center, you are here to be a master at the work that brings you the greatest joy and delight. You can and probably do work to make money and, as long as you allow Life to bring you things to respond and you follow the responses that feel amazing, you will easily and naturally tap into your abundance.

The true nature of the Sacral Center is sustainability. It takes sustainable energy to raise a family and work to provide for your family and your tribe. The Sacral Center operates in response. It is designed to give energy in response to life.

Yet sustainability is a key issue for the open Sacral Center. When you have this Center open, you don't have sustainable work force and life force energy. All Manifestors, Projectors and Reflectors have this Center open. That means that none of these Types is designed to work in the traditional way that we are conditioned to work. It also means that none of these Types has sustainable energy. If you have an open Sacral Center, you are designed to work in bursts and to also take time to rest and sustain yourself so that you stay strong, abundant and healthy.

The open Sacral Center takes in work force and life force energy and amplifies it. That means that when you have an open Sacral Center, you can sometimes feel and act like a "super" Generator. You can do more than everyone else and you feel pressure to live that out. As an open Sacral being, you can live like a "super" Generator for a finite amount of time. This is not sustainable energy for you and burnout can be a big theme in your life if you don't work in a way that sustains yourself.

The open Sacral, because it's under pressure to "work," tends to not know when enough is enough and push past what's healthy and into burnout. This burnout can be overt and obvious or subtle like boredom or even just a lack of lust for living. Either way, burnout conditions the G-Center and the magnetic monopole and, if you're burned out, you will tend to not attract anything into your life because your higher awareness knows that you need to rest and replenish yourself before your next cycle of manifestation.

The biggest fear of the open Sacral is the fear of doing "nothing." We are so deeply trained to work for money, it's often a big challenge to trust in your abundance enough to let go and allow yourself to be supported without working. Because this fear of "nothing" happening and the idea that the only way to make money is to work is so powerful, open Sacral people tend to get caught up in cycles of pushing, not knowing when enough is enough and burnout. The only way to break this cycle is to stop everything, if possible.

All people have a place, a role and the natural birthright of abundance. When you can release the fear that you are not supported and let go, it's pretty powerful to see what shows up in your life. This can be a difficult, but transformational experience for all Types, but certainly even more so for the Manifestors, Projectors and Reflectors. If you have an open Sacral, as counterintuitive as it may seem, the most powerful and abundant thing you can do sometimes is to do "nothing."

# Karen Curry Parker

## Summary

When you are struggling financially, you may feel ashamed, embarrassed and alone. My hope is that, after reading this book, you will have gained some new perspectives that help you see abundance and wealth from a newly empowered viewpoint.

This book is a simple overview of the mechanics of abundance in Human Design and represents only a slice of what you can discover about yourself and the way the world works for you. If you'd like to deepen your understanding of Human Design, check out my book, *Understanding Human Design, the New Science of Astrology: Discover Who You Really Are.*

Of course, no book can replace getting a full Human Design reading with a highly-trained Human Design Specialist. A Human Design reading will show you your specific wealth strategies and how you create an abundant, authentic life that feels good. Please visit GracePoint Matrix to find a Human Design Specialist that resonates with your specific unique design.

Even though learning the mechanics of Human Design and abundance may be new and potentially complex, it's my desire to re-emphasize a handful of simple concepts discussed throughout the book. Take them to heart and apply them in your life.

1. You are hardwired to be abundant. It's natural. No one is designed to be broke, broken, blocked or to suffer.

2. Your best bet in creating abundance in your life is to NOT use reasoning and try to figure things out with your mind. Use the power of imagining, daydreaming and visualizing possibilities to stimulate your emotions. Your emotions are your most creative energy.

3. The more you love yourself, feel powerful, embrace your uniqueness and the once-in-a-lifetime event that is YOU as well as let go of the past, get spiritually connected, take care of your body, relax and trust the flow and serve not only yourself but others, the more abundant you will be.

4. Tend to your emotional well-being with great diligence. Your emotions are your most creative source of manifesting power. Recognize how other people, your environment and your life makes you feel; if you're not feeling "good" in a situation, change your environment and change your thoughts.

5. To be abundant you must take regular cycles of rest, restoration and communion with your spiritual Source. You need to re-Source before you have resources.

6. Fear is about survival. If you're afraid to move forward in your life, push through it. The fear will dissipate. You'll grow in your confidence and ability to manifest.

7. If you are struggling, it's because you are in a cycle of growth. It will pass. Remember, we are not designed to suffer.

8. Your focus creates results. Be mindful of where you place your focus.

9. The people and the environment around you can influence you tremendously. Love yourself enough to surround yourself with people who lift you up and make you believe in the power of possibility. Make sure your energetic environment supports the unfolding of your full potential.

10. Only take actions that are in alignment with your Human Design Strategy according to your Human Design Type.

11. We ARE designed to be joyful. Relentlessly pursue your joy.

And one more thing. Imagine that your life is represented by a piece of a giant puzzle and that every person on the planet has a place in this breathtakingly beautiful image that the puzzle represents.

If you've ever put a puzzle together, you know that the beauty of the image is a result of the sum total of all of the puzzle pieces coming together. If a piece is lost, torn or jammed into the wrong place, it affects the entire face of the puzzle.

If you are a piece of this puzzle, it is your job to fill your place in the puzzle the best way you can. The more you fulfill your potential, create a life that is a manifestation of who you really are and live abundantly, the more you add to the beauty of the puzzle.

The puzzle as it exists today is what it is because of you. As you grow and change, so does everyone else. And the more you increase the abundance expressed in the puzzle, the more you increase the possibility for abundance for others in the world.

It may seem hard to imagine, but you... the REAL YOU... the You you are designed to be, have a very important and unique role in the evolution of the world. No one else can take your place.

You being the most abundant expression of yourself is the greatest contribution you can make to humanity.

# Publisher's Note

When I first discovered Human Design through Karen Curry Parker I was blown away by the accuracy and insight the system offers. I started using Human Design for myself, my family and in my business with my clients. We all saw immediate benefits - we now understood what was happening and identified what we could tweak to create more abundance in our lives.

When Karen and I started talking about her next book I knew I wanted to publish it through GracePoint Matrix, LLC.* It's not every day I get to collaborate with so many authors at the same time, all with different Designs and Strategies, and all talented and gifted.

Being a part of this book has been a total joy. Thank you so much to all the authors:

Linda Bisson Copp
Dave Buck
Linda Grace Farley
Tina Forsyth
Peg Rose Goddard
Rebekkah Hanson
Alana Heim
Sandra Lee
Evelyn Levenson
Kristin Shorter
Lorie Speciale
Quay Whitlock

I am so grateful for our Editor: Heather M. Hilliard,

Project Coordinator Camille Y. Truman, and the whole team who brought this together.

This Human Design compilation book is a collaborative effort and together, through this book, we can spread the work of Human Design to people worldwide.

If you haven't already gotten your free chart go here:
GracePointMatrix.com/Gift

To connect with our authors go here:
http://gracepointmatrix.com/abundance-by-design-book/

Enjoy creating abundance that supports your health, wealth and happiness,

Michelle Vandepas
Managing Partner
GracePoint Matrix, LLC
Publishing Division

GracePointMatrix.com Be Aligned, Purposeful, Intentional GracePoint on Facebook

*(\*Disclaimer: GracePoint LLC. is a joint collaboration with between Michelle Vandepas and Karen Curry Parker)*

CPSIA information can be obtained
at www.ICGtesting.com
Printed in the USA
BVHW051056050819
555098BV00015B/967